WORSHIP PROGRAMS
AND STORIES
FOR YOUNG PEOPLE

WORSHIP PROGRAMS AND STORIES FOR YOUNG PEOPLE

By
ALICE ANDERSON BAYS

ABINGDON-COKESBURY PRESS
NEW YORK • NASHVILLE

SET UP, PRINTED, AND BOUND BY THE
PARTHENON PRESS AT NASHVILLE, TEN-
NESSEE, UNITED STATES OF AMERICA

TO

THE YOUNG PEOPLE
WHO HAVE BEEN THE INSPIRATION
FOR THIS WORK AND TO MY SON

BOB

WHO IS A CONSTANT AND
SOMETIMES SURPRISING STIMULUS
THIS BOOK IS AFFECTIONATELY
DEDICATED

FOREWORD

THIS BOOK has grown out of an attempt to lead young people into vital worship experiences which will have an effect upon their conduct. It is not the work of one mind, but it is the result of a wide fellowship with young people in camps, in Leadership Schools, in Summer Assemblies, and in local churches. The response of these young people brought about a desire to share this material with other young people.

The worship services in Part II are not given as model services or set programs to follow, but are intended as illustrations of ways in which stories may be used to induce worship and help in the solving of some of the problems of youth. There is an urgent need for source material by which worship services may be enriched. These services are, in a small way, an answer to that need. It is hoped that they will be used to supplement, rather than take the place of, the worship suggestions of the various denominational Boards. It is also hoped that they will be suggestive of further adaptation of additional worship material. For example, the Interpretation of the Hymns in Part II indicates similar use of other hymns.

It is not the purpose of this book to discuss the nature or theory of worship. Many excellent books are available which deal adequately with that phase of the problem. In this treatise we are concerned mainly with this phase, "How stories may be used to make worship vivid and bring about desirable changes in the thinking, feeling, and acting of young people." The services included under the section "Intermediates" were planned especially for the younger adolescents. With adaptation, however, practically all the services may be used with the younger group.

I wish to acknowledge my indebtedness to the young people who have provided the incentive for the development of this material.

They not only have been the inspiration for the book, but also have furnished many valuable suggestions. To these young people, whose comradeship has been a spiritual experience, I express my deepest gratitude. To Miss Alleen Moon I wish to express my sincere appreciation for valuable suggestions concerning the arrangement of material and adaptation of stories. To Elizabeth Wray Taylor for assistance in the preparation of the material, and to Blanche Duncan Wells for reading the manuscript and for helpful criticism, I wish to express my gratitude. To my husband, whose close association with young people has given him a keen insight into their needs, I owe a debt of gratitude for valuable suggestions. The comradeship with him in young people's work has been a constant source of inspiration. It is impossible to mention all my teachers in the field of Religious Education to whom I am indebted, but I wish to acknowledge my indebtedness and express my deep appreciation and gratitude to Dr. Arlo Ayres Brown and to Dr. R. H. Edwards, who have had a large part in helping me to understand some of the problems involved in the training of young people.

Grateful acknowledgment is made to authors as well as to publishers who have granted permission for the use of copyright material. Every effort has been made to determine authorship, to trace ownership of all copyright material, and to give proper credit. The writer is not conscious of any infringement directly or indirectly. But should there be any question regarding the use of any material, the author will take pleasure in making proper acknowledgment in future editions.

This book is sent out with the earnest hope that young people may be led into a more vital relationship with God and into a more Christian way of living through the use of this material.

ALICE ANDERSON BAYS.

Kingsport, Tennessee

CONTENTS

APPENDIX

INTRODUCTION

It is easy to exhort people to worship but it requires much study and experience before one is competent to guide in worship. The author has shown herself to be a competent guide. Her experiences as a mother, a pastor's wife, and a teacher, together with painstaking study and experimentation, have given her an insight into the minds of young people so that she knows how to create together with them an atmosphere of worship and also how to guide the worship experience so that it leads to Christlike attitudes and conduct.

The reader will find in this book a wealth of material consisting of suggestions for instrumental music, together with hymns, stories, prayers, responsive readings, and other aids in worship. The stories themselves would go far to guarantee reverence and aspiration in the mind of the worshiper, but these stories are simply climatic features in services which are developed with beauty and dignity about a central theme.

Years ago while serving as president of the University of Chattanooga, it was the privilege of the writer of this Introduction to teach in many Standard Training Schools of that section. One of the students in his Chattanooga class impressed him especially by the quality of her papers and her ability to contribute helpfully to the discussions. She has through the years gone forward in the perfecting of her talents as a teacher of youth and has produced a very helpful book.

ARLO AYRES BROWN.

Drew University
Madison, New Jersey

PART ONE

WORSHIP FOR YOUNG PEOPLE

CHAPTER I

WORSHIP ADAPTED FOR YOUNG PEOPLE

"O THAT I knew where I might find Him." This ancient cry expressed the desire of man to approach God. "Here am I, send me," was Isaiah's response as he found God and dedicated himself to His service. The desire to know God is no less prevalent today, but young people are often confused when they try to find satisfaction for this urge. There are so many conceptions and ideas of worship that it is increasingly difficult for young people to find God, hear His message concerning them, and follow His leading.

Worship is a conscious effort to know God and to find His will concerning life. Any thought, feeling, or act which brings us into closer relation to God and helps us to solve our problems in the light of His presence is worship. An adequate conception of God, however, is essential for the highest type of worship. We must think of Him as a Supreme Being who inspires worship and challenges us to achieve our highest possible development.

When youth reaches the later adolescent period he begins to understand the meaning of the phrase, "lust for life." He is still in a period of physical and mental growth, yet he has matured sufficiently to strive to secure as many satisfactions as possible out of life. During this period one is apt to be confused and waste time and energy in indecision or in trial and error. The problem of the Church, of leaders of young people, and of the young people themselves is to make use of every opportunity, to realize the possibilities of life, and to utilize the idealism of youth in building right attitudes and habits in life.

There are many conditions under which one may worship. At times we are able to worship best when alone, at other times in groups.

Sometimes we find God and an answer to our problems in the presence of beauty, or in an expression of goodness. Whatever the occasion which calls forth worship, in every worship experience there should be:

(a) Realization of the presence of God,
(b) Consciousness of one's need or dependence upon God,
(c) Contemplation of the ideal or Christian way of living,
(d) Dedication or commitment of one's life to the Christian **way** of living.

MATERIALS FOR WORSHIP:

The following is a part of the resource material for worship: Scripture, prayer, hymns, poems, stories, talks, and other devotional literature. This material should be carefully selected and adapted, keeping in mind the needs of Young People, as well as their ability to understand and appreciate.

Scripture has an important place in worship. Select passages which are meaningful to the group. Omit any that are confusing or tend to detract in any way from the central idea. Lead the group in a study of devotional material with the purpose of adapting it to their own needs. Choose Scripture which is definitely related to the theme or purpose of the service.

Prayer is an intimate approach to God and should be planned with care. To have value for Young People, the prayer should express their thoughts and feelings and be true to their experiences. By using prayer to express the sentiments which have grown out of other parts of the service it may become the climax of the program.

Instrumental music may be used to prepare the group for worship. While a Prelude helps to create a worshipful attitude and centers the attention upon the purpose of the service, a Postlude may help to conserve the values of the service.

Hymn tunes should be selected which will engender worshipful emotions. They should possess real musical value, should be within the range of the vocal powers of the group, and should be in harmony with the meaning of the words of the hymn. The words should be intelligible and should express the religious aspirations of the group. They should also be in harmony with Christian ideals.

Poems have value when they are easily understood, when they

express the sentiments of the group, and when they contribute to the aim of the program. They should not be included merely for the sake of variety.

Stories or talks may be used to present the main message of the program in a vivid manner. They should be selected with a definite purpose in mind.

PRINCIPLES OF PROGRAM BUILDING:

There should be *unity* in the worship program. There should be one central aim and every element should carry forward the impression to be conveyed to the group.

Provide for *coherence*. Arrange the various parts of the program in a logical order, with each element related to the preceding one and leading to a climax.

The interest of the group should be sustained, building gradually until it has reached the highest point in the *climax*. It is important that the climax be planned with the purpose of the program in mind.

A worship service should always have *dignity*. All irrelevant material should be omitted.

Every part of the program should be *true to the experience of the group* and should be in harmony with their innermost longings.

Arrange for the *group to participate* through unison prayers, litanies, responsive readings, and hymns.

Young People should conduct their own worship services. This provides a splendid opportunity for training the group through the preparation, the discovery, and the adaptation of worship material, as well as in the actual leading of the service. Intermediates will need more supervision than the Young People. There are occasions, depending upon the nature of the program, when they may lead the service, giving the story or talk. Adult guidance will be necessary in planning details and in the choice of appropriate material. The adult leader should encourage Young People to collect worship material, guide them in the study of it, and assist them in filing it in a workable manner. In the Bibliography will be found source material which will greatly enrich the worship service

CHAPTER II

USE OF STORIES IN WORSHIP

WE USE stories, not to fill the pupil's mind with facts, but to *set him thinking*. It is necessary, however, to have sufficient knowledge to understand life in order to meet his problems successfully.

We do not use stories for the sole purpose of giving pleasure, but we use them *to present truths in a gripping manner*. The pupil may forget a certain talk, but he will remember the story which illustrated the talk. He is forming his judgments by approving or condemning the actions of the characters in the story. While these mental images are being presented to him, he is evaluating, choosing, and selecting his patterns for life.

We may use a story *to stimulate or call forth a certain feeling or attitude* on the part of the pupil. By carefully selecting our stories and by skilfully telling them we may bring about almost any reaction we desire.

It is not enough that pupils be led to form right ideals, but the imagination must be stimulated, and *they must be inspired to accomplish worthy ends*. If a story catches the fancy of a person and sets him thinking, its power for good or for evil is tremendous. Stories often provide the incentive for a vigorous fight against evil, a struggle for an inner victory, or accomplishment of a worth-while achievement.

The story is not the only means, but it is *one of the means of developing personality*. If skilfully used, it wields a powerful influence upon the lives of youthful listeners. In a story truth is presented, not as an abstract quality, but is made to live again in the life of a person. Since there is the tendency to put ourselves in the place of the characters in the story, to live vicariously in the events of the story, great care should be exercised in the selection.

What Is a Good Story?

A good short story must be an artistic product, and there are definite principles for its construction. Let us examine one of Jesus' stories, that of the prodigal son, as an example of a good story:

1. *Notice the brief introduction.* "A certain man had two sons." Jesus does not waste time in describing the characters or giving their background. In this short sentence the main characters are introduced and we begin to wonder what is going to happen to them.

2. *The action begins at once.* "The younger son said, Father, give me the portion of goods that falleth to me. And he divided unto them his living." Jesus does not stop to explain why the father gave them their inheritance. Our interest is stirred, and we want to know what happens to these sons.

3. *Interest is maintained by the plot.* Interest is increased by the introduction of one crisis after another until it reaches a high pitch. First crisis: "Not many days after the younger son took his journey into a far country, and there wasted his substance in riotous living." Another: "When he had spent all, there arose a mighty famine in that land; and he began to be in want." Finally the struggle becomes very intense as he hires himself out to feed swine, and begins to compare his condition with that of the servants in his father's house.

4. *The climax is reached when the struggle becomes the most intense.* The decision comes out of the struggle: "I will arise and go to my father."

5. *The story ends abruptly with an element of surprise.* The interest has been sustained all along, and the story closes at the highest point of interest. Notice the perfect ending of the story.

6. *Here is a splendid example of unity.* Jesus does not allow the story to trail off into unimportant happenings; no detail is introduced that is unessential. Everything has a direct bearing upon the message which Jesus describes to his hearers. Nowhere is there a better example of conciseness than in the stories of Jesus.

7. *Jesus does not tack a moral on the end of the story.* The action of the characters carries the moral ideals. There is no doubt left in the mind of his hearers concerning the message. The story shows very plainly that one way of behavior brings happiness, while another brings unhappiness.

8. *The action of the story is plausible.* The outcome of the story is

—21—

consistent with a given state of affairs. In a good story evil-doing is not made to seem alluring because it is painted realistically.

SELECTION OF STORIES:

The stage of development rather than the age of the pupil should be taken into consideration in the selection of stories. Some mature more rapidly than others, and some have had more consistent training than others. The background, as well as the growth and development, makes the pupil responsive to different types of stories.

Keep in mind certain general characteristics of young people which indicate common interests and needs. The leader should strive to minister to these needs, knowing that it is well not to overfeed any one interest to the exclusion of others. By maintaining a proper balance with stories of romance, chivalry, adventure, idealism, and service much can be done toward laying the foundation for Christian attitudes, purposes, and conceptions of life.

Stories should be true to life, even if the characters are imaginary. Do not present unnatural situations, but tell of real persons who may find it difficult always to stand steadfastly for the right.

ADAPTING STORIES:

There is a great wealth of stories; but when one begins searching for stories suitable for use in worship services for young people, there are few that can be used without changing them. Some are too long, the plot is too complicated, or there are too many characters. Others are not true to life; they may lack interest and appeal, or may be too sentimental. What may be done to adapt them for worship services?

1. *Study the story.* What is your aim in telling the story—what message do you wish to convey? Answer the following questions frankly in making your analysis of the story:

(a) Does it have all the characteristics of a good story?
(b) Is the story too long for the time in which it must be told?
(c) Are all the characters necessary to carry the impression?
(d) Are the minor scenes properly related to the major scenes?

2. *Omit any part of the story*—lengthy conversation or description —that is not essential. "Anything that does not help, hinders."

3. *Dispense with all characters* that tend to blur the scene. Sometimes, however, the lesser characters are needed as a contrast for the more important ones.

4. *Fasten each scene securely* to the preceding event. Omit any scene which would destroy the unity of the story.

5. *Focus the story* upon the impression you wish to make or the idea you desire to carry forward. Edgar Allan Poe said: "The efficient storyteller sends every ray of the story converging toward the general impression which he hopes to make."

6. *The words* which you place in the mouths of the various characters should be in harmony with the type of persons you are portraying if you change the literary style of a story. If you put other words into the mouth of the good bishop in the story, "The Bishop and the Candlesticks," let these words be in keeping with the tone of character of the bishop. Remember that every story does not need to be changed. We are apt to weaken a story by attempting to simplify the easy-flowing English of some writers.

PREPARING A STORY FOR TELLING:

It often happens that a story is told in a worship service with little or no preparation. The audience receives the impression that the whole matter is of little consequence. The best of stories may be ruined by an indifferent attitude on the part of the storyteller. How may this be overcome?

1. *Sympathy with the story is essential.* Do not attempt to tell a story unless it appeals to you personally. You should be able to feel intensely the struggle of the characters of the story.

2. *Absorb the story.* If the story does not have a message for you, it certainly will not carry one to your audience. It should possess you before you attempt to interpret it to your group. It should express, as far as possible, your own thoughts and feelings.

3. *Live with the story.* Edna Lyman in *Story-Telling* says: "Before you attempt to tell a story in the most unassuming way, live with the literature until you become filled with the spirit and atmosphere of it, and it becomes in a sense your own." Get into the mood of the story.

4. *Absorb the author's style.* To memorize a story destroys the spontaneity and often makes the telling of it mechanical. But it is possible to study the story until you can free your mind of the sentence construction and think only of the message you wish to transmit.

5. *Study the background of the story* until you know something of the history of the period, the customs and characteristics of the people.

6. *Inner visualization is important.* Live with the story until you can see the scenes moving before you as in a silent drama.

TELLING THE STORY:

The personality of the storyteller helps to interpret the message. Jesus' stories gripped the hearts of his hearers because he embodied in his own life the principles which he taught. What you are either helps or hinders your message.

1. *Forget yourself.* Concentrate—bring all your powers to focus upon one point, and it will enable you to bring the message with greater force. If there is pretense or imitation, however, it will be detected by your audience. Keep in mind the difference between the storyteller and the dramatic reader. The storyteller is describing action, while the dramatic reader is acting out the story.

2. *The posture is important.* See that your entire being responds to the appeal of the story. The expression of the face as well as the tone of voice should be in harmony with the mood of the story. There should be no jarring mannerisms, or anything that would attract attention to the storyteller.

3. *Give the story in direct discourse.* Let your characters talk. Suppose that Jesus had said, "And the son, when he came to himself, said that he would arise and go to his father." How much more effective it is to say: "I will arise and go to my father." [1]

PART TWO

SERVICES OF WORSHIP

GROUP I

Biographical

SERVICE I: FREEDOM OF TRUTH

AIM: To challenge the group to the adventure of the quest for truth.

INSTRUMENTAL PRELUDE: *"Elegie"* (MASSENET).

CALL TO WORSHIP:

> Surely the Lord is in this place.
> This is none other but the house of the Lord
>   and the gate to heaven.

> O come, let us worship and bow down,
> Let us kneel before the Lord our Maker.

HYMN: *"O Life That Maketh All Things New."*

SCRIPTURE:

O send out thy light and thy truth; let them lead me;
Let them bring me to thy holy hill,
And to thy tabernacles.

When he, the Spirit of truth, is come,
He will guide you into all truth.

Ye shall know the truth,
And the truth shall make you free.

Study to shew thyself approved unto God,
A workman that needeth not to be ashamed,
Rightly dividing the word of truth.[2]

PRAYER:

O Christ, the way, the truth, the life,
    Show me the living way,
That in the tumult and the strife,
    I may not go astray.

Teach me Thy truth, O Christ, my light,
    The truth that makes me free,
That in the darkness and the night
    My trust shall be in Thee.

The life that Thou alone canst give,
    Impart in love to me,
That I may in Thy presence live,
    And ever be like Thee.

—GEORGE L. SQUIER.

STORY:

"THE TIRELESS SEARCHER" [3]

ONE DAY in October, 1831, a boy aged nine ran away from a crowd which surrounded a blacksmith's shop, where the victims of a mad wolf were undergoing the agony of having their mangled flesh cauterized. The screams of these victims rang in his ears for days, and the iron which seared the wounds left upon Louis Pasteur a vivid impression which he was never able to forget. It was probably this incident which led him to devote the best years of his life to a search for the truth concerning microbes.

When Pasteur was twenty years old he entered the normal school in Paris to specialize in chemistry. At first he showed no signs of becoming a great scientist. The professor who wrote "mediocre" on his entrance papers was probably astonished later at the accomplishments of his pupil, for at the early age of twenty-six Pasteur made his first important discovery concerning the tiny crystals which form in wine.

Later as Professor and Dean of the Faculty of Science in Lille he began an intensive search for the truth concerning microbes. Night after night he worked feverishly, following false leads, running into blind alleys, seeking the truth which eluded him. Contrary to the general belief at that time, he set out to prove that microbes must have parents, that life springs from existing life, and not from life-less matter.

In his efforts to help the wine growers he found that some germs are friendly, while others are deadly enemies of mankind. Fermentation was caused by certain microbes, but the presence of other germs caused the wine to turn sour. After making many experiments, he found that, by gently heating the mixture, the intruding germs could be killed, and the fermentation would proceed naturally. This is the process which is known today as "pasteurizing."

Because microbes were so small, many scientists of that day thought it impossible to obtain accurate information about them, but Pasteur was determined to bring them out of their obscurity. He knew that they were always present, causing milk to sour, the butter to become rancid, and the meat to putrefy; but the question which baffled him was: Where did they come from:

Day after day he spent making experiments which were very trying, but his work was ennobled because it was in the interest of humanity. He finally came to the conclusion that the dust in the air carried germs which were the cause of disease, and the idea came to him: Why not wipe out all germs and free the world of disease?

Many of the doctors at that time objected to Pasteur invading their territory. They reasoned: "What right does this chemist have to undertake to tell us the cause of disease? It is true we do not know, but we will not be told by a chemist." Lister, the famous English surgeon, was an exception. He gave Pasteur credit for discovering the principle which made the antiseptic system a success. By using this idea in his surgery, Lister was able to operate with less danger of infection.

Pasteur now stumbled upon an idea which proved to be his greatest contribution to mankind, that of using living microbes to fight each other. He worked frantically until he perfected a vaccine which was effective in the treatment of cholera and anthrax. He was so sure of himself that he announced his vaccine for anthrax to the Academy of Science in Paris, but was challenged to prove the effectiveness of it by a public demonstration. In agreeing, he proposed to inoculate twenty-five sheep or cattle, and thus immunize them against the disease, while another twenty-five would remain untreated. The deadly anthrax bacilli would be given to all of them alike.

The experiment was a complete success, for not one of the animals that had been vaccinated was affected in the least by the dose of anthrax, while all the unprotected ones lay dead in the field. It was a great day for Pasteur! He believed that he was giving a demonstration of one of the finest examples of applied science the world had ever seen. A step forward had been made in man's fight against relentless nature. Even the skeptics were convinced!

Pasteur was not content, however, to stop with this victory. That harrowing scene around the blacksmith's shop was still vivid in his memory. Surely there must be some way of finding a cure for hydrophobia. As he set himself to this task, he and his assistants performed experiments which would have discouraged less courageous men, but they continued until they found a vaccine which proved successful when tried on dogs and rabbits.

The question confronting Pasteur was: Will it prove as effective on human beings? He was so sure of it that he was inclined to try it on himself. But this experiment was not necessary, for on July 6, 1885, a woman came begging him to treat her son who had been bitten two days before by a mad dog. Pasteur finally consented, and that night the first injection for rabies was made in a human body. The injections were continued for fourteen days consecutively. Then the boy went home without a trace of the disease.

The news of the boy's recovery spread until victims of rabies began to pour in from many corners of the world. From Russia there came nineteen peasants who had been bitten by a mad wolf nineteen days before. The disease had made such headway that injections were made twice a day to make up for lost time, and all but three of the victims were saved.

Upon their return to Russia a great shout of praise went up from all the world. Mankind had been freed of this dread disease. The wave of enthusiasm spread until money began to pour in from many unexpected places. The Czar of Russia sent one hundred thousand francs; others added to this sum until there were millions of francs. Pasteur set to work to build a suitable laboratory, which was the beginning of the Pasteur Institute. Today similar institutes may be found in every country.

France honored this great man in 1892 on his seventieth birthday with a celebration at the Sorbonne in Paris to which many famous men were invited. This tireless worker had been so zealous in his efforts to save human life that he had little energy left for this occasion. The speech which he had written had to be read by another. His remarks were directed to the students present, advising them to consider the purpose of their lives, and the contribution they might give to their country in return for their education. He stressed the fact, which was a firm conviction of his, that happiness comes to those who contribute in some way to the welfare and progress of humanity. His last words to them were a Hymn of Hope, not so much for the saving of life, but for the losing of one's life in self-sacrifice and devotion to the service of mankind.

LITANY OF THANKSGIVING:

Leader: For the steady advance of civilization, for the pioneers and other great leaders who have helped to make our civilization possible,
Response: Father, we thank Thee.
Leader: For Thy humble servants, the scientists who have given themselves to a search for truth,
Response: Father, we thank Thee.
Leader: For all other seekers of truth who have learned to think Thy thoughts after Thee, and have dedicated their abilities to the service of mankind,
Response: We humbly thank Thee, O God.
Leader: For all the discoveries that have freed us from disease, relieved us of burdens, and added to the enjoyment of life,
Response: We thank Thee, O God.
Leader: For all those unselfish seekers who have labored so zealously that we might enjoy a fuller life,
Response: We thank Thee, O God.
Leader: Grant unto us a vision of things we can do in bringing greater freedom to mankind; and may we dedicate ourselves to a search for truth.
Response: We humbly pray in Jesus' name. AMEN.

HYMN: *"Pass on the Torch."* [4]

GROUP I

Biographical

SERVICE II: GLORIFYING THE COMMONPLACE

AIM: To lead the group to realize that God is revealed in the common things of life and that one may serve Him by doing faithfully the simple tasks near at hand.

INSTRUMENTAL PRELUDE: Andante from the New World Symphony (DVORAK).

CALL TO WORSHIP:

> Light of the world, before Thee
> Our spirits prostrate fall;
> We worship, we adore Thee,
> Thou Light, the life of all;
> With Thee is no forgetting
> Of all Thine hand hath made;
> Thy rising hath no setting,
> Thy sunshine hath no shade.
>
> Light of the world, illumine
> This darkened earth of Thine
> Till everything that's human
> Be filled with the divine;
> Till every tongue and nation,
> From sin's dominion free,
> Rise in the new creation
> Which springs from love and Thee.
> —JOHN S. B. MONSELL.

HYMN: *"My God, I Thank Thee, Who Hast Made."*

RESPONSIVE READING:

Leader: Let us now praise famous men, and our fathers that begat us.

Response: The Lord manifested in them great glory; even His mighty power from the beginning.

Leader: Leaders of the people by their counsels, and by their understanding men of learning for the people, wise and eloquent in their instructions:

Response: Rich men furnished with ability, living peaceably in their habitations:

Leader: All these were honored in their generations, and were the glory of their times.

Response: There be some of them that have left a name behind them to declare their praises. And some there be, who have no memorial; who are perished, as though they had never been.

Leader: But these were men of mercy, whose righteous deeds have not been forgotten.

Response: Their bodies are buried in peace; and their name liveth evermore. The people will tell of their wisdom, and the congregation will show forth their praise.[5]

STORY:

"GLORIFYING THE COMMONPLACE"[6]

DR. GEORGE WASHINGTON CARVER is one of the remarkable men of this age. His life reads like that of the most romantic characters in fiction. Born in slavery with obstacles almost insurmountable, he has climbed to a position of equality with the foremost scientists of the world. Probably no group of scientists today would deny him a place among them. He has won this position because he is a pioneer in a new field, his explorations in agricultural chemistry being among the first in that area.

Dr. Carver's achievements are all the more remarkable when they are considered against the background of his ancestry. He was born of slave parents near the close of the War between the States, at a time when no Negroes were entirely safe. He and his mother were stolen by nightriders and taken from their home on the farm of Moses Carver in Missouri to Arkansas. The lad was rescued by a party of men who exchanged an old racehorse for him, but he never saw his mother again. When restored to the Carvers he was suffering from exposure which left him rather frail. Consequently, he was not expected to do much work, so he spent his time roving about the farm gathering queer flowers and weeds. This was the beginning of his interest in plants.

Dr. Carver worked his way through high school and college, earning the degree of Master of Science, and later was honored with the degree of Doctor of Science. In Iowa State College the authorities were so impressed with his work that at graduation he was given a place on the college faculty, where he taught until Booker T. Washington invited him to come to Tuskegee Institute.

Here was the opportunity he had been wanting: the chance to serve his own people. His students came from poor families that grew some sweet potatoes and a few peanuts. He began experimenting to find out what products could be taken from these common crops. He believes that the greatest opportunities for enriching the world lie in the field of synthetic chemistry. In his laboratory he has developed over two hundred commercial by-products of the peanut, and has done almost the same with the sweet potato. The pecan has furnished him with eighty discoveries. He has done more with the peanut, however, than with anything else. Eventually his achievements in this field may prove to be the most valuable to the world.

Dr. Carver has found that nature has stored in the peanut the finest of food materials. He has explored this storehouse until many of its secrets have been revealed. The products are so numerous as to tax one's powers to remember them all. He began his research by producing from the peanut milk which is so natural that the cream rises on it as it does on real milk. And he explains that it is good Jersey milk and not "boarding-house milk" either. By this discovery the lives of many Negro children in Africa have been saved. It is very difficult to keep cows alive in certain sections of Africa, but peanuts can be grown there very easily. Naturally the poorer children never had any milk until Dr. Carver's discovery.

The peanut has yielded scientific marvels ranging all the way from foods to dyes, wood stains, face powder, and ink. In his laboratory one may see an ice cream mixture from which delicious ice cream can be made; preparations for making candies; cocoa, chocolate bars, and caramels; instant coffee which already has cream and sugar in it; sauces and oil for various purposes; shaving lotions; a rubbing oil that is said to have remarkable properties; lard, linoleum, rubber, axle grease, face powder, and soap. All are made from the peanut and labeled with the ink made from the same lowly product. Dr. Carver says that he has merely scratched the surface of possibilities in creative chemistry, and that some day he hopes to ask the Creator this question: "What else can be made from the peanut?"

Dr. Carver has many experiments under way all the time and is continually starting something new, yet he is never too busy to escort the visitor through his laboratory and explain his products. Probably it is because of his modesty that his research work is not better known. He usually begins by showing the visitor some pieces of pottery, apologizing for their crudeness, saying that he is not a potter. He points out that the South has some of the finest pottery clays to be found in the world; yet little has been realized from this resource.

Dr. Carver's work has been with the commonplace things about him. From the clays he has produced over one hundred tints and shades of colors, among them a beautiful blue which closely resembles that found in the tomb of King Tutankhamen. This may prove to be a rediscovery of the process known to the Egyptians of making permanent colors. The question usually asked by the visitor about the colors is: "Will they fade?" Dr. Carver's reply is: "Why should they? They have been lying here in the hills for centuries with colors unchanged; why should they fade when taken out of the ground?" One is struck with the unusual quality of Dr. Carver's paints when compared with those on the market.

One of the most valuable of Dr. Carver's products is his synthetic marble, which is made from wood shavings and other waste materials. It has all the appearance of real marble, is strong and substantial, and takes a high polish. Other common things usually thought of as waste products have been turned into useful commodities. From peanut hulls he has made insulating boards for houses; from okra fiber he has made rope; from tomato vines he has made dyes; and he has even made the leaves and muck of swamps yield valuable fertilizer. From the roots of the Florida palm he has made, in natural colors, synthetic wood which can be used for interior woodwork and for furniture.

As Dr. Carver has wrested these secrets from nature, he has given them freely to the world, asking nothing in return except that they be used for the benefit of mankind. He has not been concerned about marketing his products; that is left for those who have capital to invest. He has never cared for money; most of his salary has been used to educate deserving boys. Some wealthy peanut growers in Florida had benefited by his advice concerning a disease which was affecting their crops. After his treatment eradicated the disease, they sent him a check which he courteously returned.

In conversation with Dr. Carver one is impressed with the quality of his mind, the extent of his knowledge, and his deep humility. His great mental capacity marks him as a genius, yet he is the most modest of men. At times he gives the impression of being very timid. He has, however, a most engaging personality, a voice that is remarkably expressive, and eyes that twinkle and smile. One cannot look into his kindly face without seeing the unmistakable spiritual quality of his life. He is a very devout man with a simple faith in God. He speaks of the secrets which he has discovered as "God's secrets," and often refers to himself as "God's Interpreter." He says: "Man is endowed with an intellect which he is to use in searching out the secrets of nature; and if he will keep in tune with God, many of these secrets will be revealed to him."

Most people are content to excel in one field; but here is a man who is not only a botanist, chemist, and scientist, but also a musician, an artist, and an educator. How does he find time to carry on his many lines of work? The explanation is probably that he is up as early as four o'clock every morning. It is in these early hours when he is unmolested that he works with the things of nature that he loves so well, and over which he is so complete a master. It is at this time that he carries on his experimental work.

Having no family, Dr. Carver lives alone in two rooms, one of which is his bedroom, the other his "den." Many objects of his own handiwork—such as pottery, paintings, sketches of rare flowers, and pieces of crochet work which he delights to do in his spare moments—may be seen in his den. There is one piece of furniture which is his most cherished possession: a spinning wheel which was used by his mother in the days of slavery. Under no consideration would he part with it. When his mother was stolen by nightriders he was too young to realize what it meant; when he grew older he carried on an extensive search for years, but never found any trace of her. This spinning wheel is his only connection with his mother and the past; so, when he touches it, he does it reverently and tenderly.

Many honors have come to this simple, humble man. Because of his remarkable discoveries tempting offers have come to him, one of which was when Thomas A. Edison invited him to come to his New Jersey laboratory at a salary of $100,000 per year. In refusing this offer Dr. Carver said: "Booker T. Washington placed me here nearly twenty-five years ago, and told me to let down my bucket, so I have always tried to do that, and it has never failed to come up full of sparkling water. My work is here in the South, and I believe that my own race should benefit from my discoveries."

POEM: *"Seek Not Afar for Beauty"*

Seek not afar for beauty: lo, it glows
In dew-wet grasses all about thy feet;
In birds, in sunshine, childish faces sweet,
In stars and mountain summits topped with snows.

Go not abroad for happiness: for, see,
It is a flower blooming at thy door.
Bring love and justice home, and then no more
Thou'll wonder in what dwelling joy may be.

Dream not of noble service elsewhere wrought;
The simple duty that awaits thy hand
Is God's voice uttering a divine command;
Life's common deeds build all that saints have thought.

In wonder workings, or some bush aflame,
Men look for God and fancy Him concealed:
But in earth's common things He stands revealed,
While grass and flowers and stars spell out His name.
—MINOT J. SAVAGE.

LITANY OF THANKSGIVING:

Leader: For the great men of all ages who have lived so close to Thee, that they have been able to think Thy thoughts after Thee,

Response: We give Thee thanks, O God.

Leader: For the scientists to whom Thou hast revealed Thy secrets, and for their unselfishness which has led them to labor unceasingly for the common good of all,

Response: Accept our thanks, O God.

Leader: For this great servant of Thine, who has been content to work with the commonplace things of life, the things which we ordinarily pass by unnoticed,

Response: Accept our grateful thanks, O God.

Leader: For his unselfishness in passing on to others without hope of any reward the secrets which he has learned from Thee,

Response: We thank Thee for his noble example.

Leader: Save us from selfish ambitions which would cause us to seek the applause of men and material gains.

Response: Deliver us from low desires.

Leader: Grant unto us the insight into the power of a life devoted to a search for truth, and to the service of humanity.

Response: Hear us, O God, we beseech Thee.

Leader: Help us to understand that the least of us may be interpreters of Thy truth in the world if we are but willing to live according to Thy purpose.

UNISON PRAYER:

God of all Wisdom, Thou hast hidden Thy truth that only those who thirst for it can find it. Forgive us for our impatient complaint at not finding Thy secrets lying at the roadside awaiting us, in our ignorant and careless wanderings. We thank Thee, O God, that Thou hast ordained an inner unity of spirit between Thy truth and those who are to see it. Grant us the ability to enjoy facts. Teach us the joy that comes from tracing Thy footsteps in the holy pathway between Cause and Effect. Let us stand humbly beneath the Stars, silently beside a Test Tube, patiently before an expanding Purpose in Society, with an inquiring mind at the Doorway of Literature, reverently before a Growing Life. Stretch our souls up to the capacity that would make us Thy Spiritual Pioneers. Give us a thirst for Truth. When Truth wrecks our complacency, disturbs our prejudices, sets us afloat on a strange sea, O God, keep us athirst for more. In the name of Him who is the Truth and the Life. AMEN.[7]

HYMN: *"Pass on the Torch,"* or
　　　"O Jesus, Prince of Life and Truth," or
　　　"O Master Workman of the Race."

— 38 —

BENEDICTION:

Father, give Thy benediction,
  Give Thy peace before we part;
Still our minds with truth's conviction;
  Calm with trust each anxious heart.
Let Thy voice with sweet commanding,
  Bid our grief and struggles end;
Peace which passeth understanding
  On our waiting spirits send.
                —SAMUEL LONGFELLOW.

GROUP I

Biographical

SERVICE III: ACCEPTING LIMITATIONS

AIM: To lift up in the thinking of the group the necessity of facing limitations courageously and developing one's talents to the fullest extent.

INSTRUMENTAL PRELUDE: *"Moonlight Sonata"* (BEETHOVEN, violin and piano).

SALUTATION:

> All people that on earth do dwell,
> Sing to the Lord with cheerful voice.
> Him serve with mirth, His praise forth tell;
> Come ye before Him and rejoice.
>
> O enter then His gates with praise,
> Approach with joy His courts unto;
> Praise, laud, and bless His Name always,
> For it is seemly so to do.
> —WILLIAM KETHE.

RESPONSIVE READINGS:

Leader: Behold, I have set before thee this day life and good, and death and evil;

Response: In that I command thee this day to love the Lord thy God, to walk in his way.

Leader: Keep thy heart with all diligence; for out of it are the issues of life.

Response: Trust in the Lord with all thine heart; and lean not unto thine own understanding.

Leader: In all thy ways acknowledge him, and he shall direct thy paths.

Response: I count not myself to have apprehended: but this one thing I do, forgetting those things which are behind, and reaching forth unto those things which are before, I press toward the mark for the prize of the high calling of God in Christ Jesus.

Leader: Let us lay aside every weight, and the sin which doth so easily beset us,

Response: And let us run with patience the race that is set before us; looking unto Jesus, the author and finisher of our faith.[8]

UNISON PRAYER (to be sung to tune "Southampton"):

> Father in heaven, hear us today;
> Hallowed Thy name be, hear us, we pray.
> O let Thy kingdom come,
> O let Thy will be done,
> By all beneath the sun,
> As in the skies.
>
> Father in heaven, hear us today;
> Hallowed Thy name be, hear us, we pray.
> Giver of daily food,
> Fountain of truth and good,
> Be all our hearts imbued
> With love like Thine.
>
> Father in heaven, hear us today;
> Hallowed Thy name be, hear us, we pray.
> Lead us in paths of right,
> Save us from sin and blight,
> King of all love and might,
> Glorious for aye.
> —CHARLES GORDON AMES.

OFFERTORY:

Leader: Let us remember the words of Christ himself who said: It is more blessed to give than to receive.

HYMN: *"Be Strong! We Are Not Here to Play."*

STORY:

"THE WHITTLER OF CREMONA" [9]

IT WAS Maytime and Cremona was gay in fantastic attire, for it was the last day of carnival week. In a narrow alley-like street three boys were standing in the shadows. They had no part in the merriment. Perhaps they had left the throng because of their somber attire; or to talk over a question that seemed important, for two of them were in earnest conversation, while the third stood quietly by, whittling at a piece of stick. He was younger than the others, with a sensitive face and big, expressive eyes. His companions called him Tonio.

"But I tell you, Salvator, every minute lost now is like throwing gold away. People are generous at carnival time, for a merry heart makes an open hand."

"Perhaps you are right, Gulio. Shall we start now?"

"Yes, to the piazza, in front of the cathedral, where a crowd is always passing. You sing, and I will play. Do you want to go, too, Tonio?"

Antonio looked up from the stick that was beginning to take the semblance of a dagger under his knife. "Yes, I'd like to be with you, even if I cannot sing."

"You certainly cannot sing; you can do nothing but whittle, which is a pity, for that never turns a penny your way. But hurry."

The brothers chatted as they went along, but Antonio said little. Gulio's remark that he could do nothing but whittle was still in his mind; and while he knew it to be true, it made him sad. He loved music, yet he had no part in making it. When he tried to sing his voice squeaked so that the boys laughed. It was hard to be just a whittler when his companions could play and sing so well.

Soon they were in front of the great cathedral, where a throng continually moved by. Without losing a minute Gulio took his violin from its case and began the prelude of a Lombardian folk song. Salvator's voice was sweet and flutelike. And as he sang several stopped to listen, and dropped coins into his hand when he had finished.

A man walked by and, seeing the youthful musicians, came close to where they stood. "That is a pretty song, lad. Would you sing it again to please a lonely man's fancy?" He stood with half-closed eyes and seemed to hear nothing but the music. Then, handing Salvator a coin, he went down the street without noticing Antonio, who still sat whittling on the steps.

Salvator held up the coin in the waning light and gave a cry: "A gold piece! A gold piece for a song!" Gulio looked at him dubiously. But when he examined it, he exclaimed: "Truly a gold piece! But he can afford it. That is the great Amati."

Antonio came and looked at the money and asked, "Who is Amati, and why do you call him great?"

Salvator stared in amazement: "You have not heard of Amati?"

Before he could answer Gulio interrupted: "Of course not. Antonio is just a whittler. He knows about knives and woods, but little about music. Amati is a violin maker, the greatest in Italy and very rich. Yet men say he cares for nothing in the world but his work."

The brothers were so happy over their money that they wanted to get home. Since Antonio had no desire to be there alone, he went to his own home and crept to bed. But he did not sleep, for his brain was afire with a thought that had just come into it. He could not sing; he could do nothing but whittle, and here in his own Cremona was a man who with knives and wood made wonderful violins.

Before dawn next day he was up. He crept out of the house while his parents were still asleep and took with him some things he had made with his knife. Somewhere in the city the master violin maker dwelt, and he meant to find him. It was not long until Antonio stood at his door. The servant scolded him away, because he disturbed the house so early. So he waited in the street until it was time for work to begin, when again he rapped on the door. Again the servant was about to drive him away, when the Master came to the door.

"I have brought these things for you to see," Antonio said; "I cut them with my knife, and I want to know if you think I can learn to make violins."

The great man smiled: "What is your name, lad?"

"Antonio Stradivarius."

"And why do you want to make violins?"

"Because I love music and cannot make any. My companions can both sing and play. You heard them last night in the piazza in front of the cathedral and gave them the gold piece. I love music as much as they, but my voice is squeaky. I can do nothing but whittle."

"Come into the house and you shall try. The song in the heart is all that matters, for there are many ways of making music. Some play violins, some sing, some paint pictures and make statues, while others till the soil and make flowers bloom. Each sings a song and helps to make music for the world. If you put your best into it, the song you sing with knives and wood will be just as noble as the one Salvator and Gulio sing with voice and violin."

So Antonio became a pupil of the great Amati. Day after day he toiled in the workshop, until at last he had a violin. It was not done in a day or a month, for the Master taught him many lessons besides those in cutting and shaping and string-placing, one of which was that a tiny bit of work well done each day is what means great achievement in the end. Sometimes he wanted to hurry and work less carefully than his teacher advised, but gradually he learned that patience is worth more than all things else to him who would excel.

Antonio kept steadily on at his much-loved work, trying to make each violin better and more beautiful than the one before it. As the years passed his violins became known all over Italy. Musicians said their tone was marvelously sweet and mellow, and wondered how it could be. But to Antonio it seemed very simple; it was just because he put so much love into the making.

That was over two hundred years ago; and now, at the mention of Cremona, men think not of the fair city beside the Po, whose stately cathedral still looks out over the fertile plains of Lombardy, but of the world's greatest violin-maker, Antonio Stradivarius, who with a song in his heart found another way of singing it.

PRAYER:

O Thou who art the Father of us all, we humble ourselves as we wait in Thy presence. The sense of our shortcomings is before us; forgive us for our weaknesses, and pardon our mistakes. At times our strength is not sufficient for the tasks that await us, but we would avail ourselves of the power which comes from communion with Thee. We are grateful to Thee for the talents with which Thou hast endowed us. Help us to realize that each of us has a contribution to make and grant that we may determine to put our best efforts into whatever work our hands find to do. Give us wisdom to select the work which we are by nature best fitted to do; teach us the sacredness of honest labor; and grant that we may devote our strength to the common good of all Thy children. We ask these things in the name of Jesus. AMEN.

HYMN: *"Awake, Awake to Love and Work."*

BENEDICTION:

> Be with us, God the Father,
> Be with us, God the Son,
> Be with us, God the Spirit,
> Eternal Three in One!
> Make us a royal priesthood,
> Thee rightly to adore,
> And fill us with Thy fulness
> Now and forevermore.
> —JOHN S. B. MONSELL.

GROUP II

Christian Living

SERVICE IV: THE SECURITY OF INNER PEACE

AIM: To lead to a greater desire to find harmony and peace within oneself through fellowship with God.

INSTRUMENTAL PRELUDE: *"Consolation,"* from "Song without Words," Op. 30, No. 3 (MENDELSSOHN).

CALL TO WORSHIP:

> Lift up your heads, ye mighty gates!
> Behold the King in glory waits,
> The Prince of Peace is drawing near,
> The hope of longing hearts is here;
> The end of all our woe He brings,
> Wherefore the earth is glad and sings.
>
> Fling wide the portals of your heart!
> Make it a temple, set apart
> From earthly use for heaven's employ,
> Adorned with prayer and love and joy;
> So shall your Sovereign enter in,
> And new and nobler life begin.
> —GEORGE WEISSEL.

HYMN: *"Lead Us, O Father, in the Paths of Peace,"* or
"The King of Love My Shepherd Is,"
"When Peace Like a River,"
"Saviour, Again to Thy Dear Name."

RESPONSIVE READING:

Leader: Mark the perfect man, and behold the upright: for the end of that man is peace.[10]

Response (to be sung):

> Dear Lord and Father of mankind,
> Forgive our foolish ways;
> Reclothe us in our rightful mind,
> In purer lives Thy service find,
> In deeper reverence, praise.[11]

Leader: Blessed are the peacemakers: for they shall be called the children of God.[10]

Response:

> In simple trust like theirs who heard,
> Beside the Syrian sea,
> The gracious calling of the Lord,
> Let us, like them, without a word
> Rise up and follow Thee.[11]

Leader: Peace I leave with you, my peace I give unto you: not as the world giveth, give I unto you.[10]

Response:

> O Sabbath rest by Galilee!
> O calm of hills above,
> Where Jesus knelt to share with Thee
> The silence of eternity,
> Interpreted by love! [11]

Leader: Let not your heart be troubled, neither let it be afraid.[10]

Response:

> Drop Thy still dews of quietness,
> Till all our strivings cease;
> Take from our souls the strain and stress,
> And let our ordered lives confess
> The beauty of Thy peace.[11]

Leader: These things have I spoken unto you, that in me ye might have peace.[10]

Response:

Breathe through the heats of our desire
   Thy coolness and Thy balm;
Let sense be dumb, let flesh retire;
Speak through the earthquake, wind, and fire,
   O still small voice of calm! [11]

Poem:

"I Look to Thee in Every Need"

I look to Thee in every need,
   And never look in vain;
I feel Thy strong and tender love,
   And all is well again:
The thought of Thee is mightier far
Than sin and pain and sorrow are.

Thy calmness bends serene above,
   My restlessness to still;
Around me glows Thy quickening life,
   To nerve my faltering will:
Thy presence fills my solitude;
Thy providence turns all to good.
     —SAMUEL LONGFELLOW.

Story:

"THE LATCHSTRING" [12]

"Well, perhaps we ought at least to bar our door, for the sake of the children." Mary Tyler spoke reluctantly, and there was a note of uncertainty in her voice.

"Perhaps so," replied James Tyler. "It seems to me every man within five miles has upbraided me for not protecting my children."

Mary glanced with troubled eyes at the face of her husband, as they sat before the fire in their little cabin. She knew that he, too, was living over the uncertain days since the outbreak of the war. Time and again there had been reports that the British soldiers had incited the Indians to burn the cabins of the settlers and massacre whole families.

Despite these reports, the Tylers had lived, as before, on friendly terms with their neighbors, both Indians and white men. When massacres had occurred in nearby settlements, they had still continued to leave out the latchstring—that leather thong which enabled a person outside the door to lift the latch and enter.

The Tylers had trusted entirely to the protection of their Heavenly Father, and had refused to arm themselves, or even to lock the door. Now they had reliable assurance that the Indians were coming to destroy their settlement. Neighbors urged that they had no right to imperil the lives of their children by such foolhardiness; that they should protect themselves.

"But is it really protection?" Mary queried, as they sat alone in their cabin.

"At least," responded James, "we shall be doing what most people consider safest."

For what seemed a long time, they sat gazing at the fire. The silence was broken only by the moaning of the wind in the pine trees and the crackling of the logs on the hearth. For the first time in all the dark days, Mary felt afraid. She stirred uneasily and cast a furtive glance around the shadowy room. James rose and lighted a candle. He crossed the room and stood for a moment uncertainly beside the outside door. Then, with a deep sigh, he pulled in the leather thong, fastened the latch securely, and prepared for bed.

All night James tossed restlessly. Every time one of the children stirred, or a branch scraped the roof, he would start violently, and fall back unnerved. He tried to calm himself by repeating verses from the Bible, but instead of the usual comfort, the words only brought a challenge to his excited brain: "Why are ye fearful, O ye of little faith?" "Take the shield of faith, wherewith ye shall be able to quench all the fiery darts of the wicked."

"Mary," he whispered at last, "are you awake?"

"Yes, James," she replied, "I have not slept. I have tried to pray, and always the answer has been, 'Behold, the Lord's hand is not shortened that it cannot save.'"

"You are right, Mary, the Lord's hand is not shortened that it cannot save, and we did wrong to pull in the latchstring. Shall we put our trust in Him entirely?"

"Yes, James, I should feel much safer so," she replied. Quickly James stepped to the door and pulled the leather thong through to the outside. Then he lay down again, and both enjoyed a security that they had not felt for hours.

Suddenly, just as they were about to drop off to sleep, they heard

— 49 —

a bloodcurdling warwhoop. A few seconds later the moccasined footsteps of several men passed the window and stopped in front of the door. The latch clicked and the door swung open. By the dim light from the embers on the hearth, James could see seven Indians in full war paint. They motioned and talked to each other and then silently pulled the door to and disappeared into the night.

In the morning, when James and Mary looked out of their door, they saw only the smoking ruins of their neighbors' cabins.

Years later, when the war was over, the government of the United States appointed James Tyler as a representative to an Indian conference. One day he told this story to all those assembled. In reply an Indian arose and said:

"I was one of those Indians. We crept up in the night. We meant to burn and kill. We found the latchstring out. We said, 'No burn this house; no kill these people; they do us no harm; they trust the Great Spirit.'"

POEM: *"'Mid All the Traffic of the Ways"* [13]
              'Mid all the traffic of the ways,
                  Turmoils without, within,
              Make in my heart a quiet place,
                  And come and dwell therein:

              A little shrine of quietness,
                  All sacred to Thyself,
              Where Thou shalt all my soul possess,
                  And I may find myself:

              A little shelter from life's stress,
                  Where I may lay me prone,
              And bare my soul in loneliness,
                  And know as I am known:

              A little place of mystic grace,
                  Of self and sin swept bare,
              Where I may look upon Thy face,
                  And talk with Thee in prayer.
                          —JOHN OXENHAM.

PRAYER:
     O Eternal Father, author of all peace, worker of all righteousness, and ruler of all people, we come before Thee in the spirit of the eager

searcher for truth. Thine arm has never failed us and Thy strength has been sufficient for our every need. Grant unto us a faith which will enable us to trust our lives to Thy leadership. We sometimes become so engrossed in the cares of everyday living that we fail to hear Thy voice. Create within us a greater desire for communion with Thee, and increase our capacity for fellowship with Thee. Give unto us peace which the world cannot give. In Jesus' name we ask these blessings. AMEN.

SOLO: "Come unto Me" (to tune of "Adrian").

> Come unto me, when shadows darkly gather,
>   When the sad heart is weary and distressed;
> Seeking for comfort from your Heavenly Father,
>   Come unto me, and I will give you rest.
>
> There, like an Eden blossoming in gladness,
>   Bloom the fair flowers the earth too rudely pressed;
> Come unto me, all ye who droop in sadness,
>   Come unto me, and I will give you rest.
>   —CATHERINE H. ESLING.

BENEDICTION:

May the God of peace make you perfect in every good work to do His will, through Jesus Christ. AMEN.

GROUP II

Christian Living

SERVICE V: COMRADES ALONG THE WAY

AIM: To lead to an awareness of the value of friendship.

INSTRUMENTAL PRELUDE: *"Cavatina"* (RAFF, violin and piano selection).

CALL TO WORSHIP:

> This is the day which the Lord hath made.
> Let us rejoice and be glad in it.
> O come, let us worship and bow down;
> Let us kneel before the Lord our Maker;
> He is our God, and we are the people of
>   his pasture and the sheep of his hand.

HYMN: *"Heaven Is Here, Where Hymns of Gladness."*

SCRIPTURE:

This is my commandment, That ye love one another, as I have loved you. Greater love hath no man than this, that a man lay down his life for his friends. Ye are my friends, if ye do whatsoever I command you. Henceforth I call you not servants; for the servant knoweth not what his lord doeth: but I have called you friends; for all things that I have heard of my father I have made known unto you.[14]

PRAYER:

> Father of men, in whom are one
> All humankind beneath Thy sun,
> Stablish our work in Thee begun.
> Except the house be built of Thee,

In vain the builder's toil must be:
O strengthen our infirmity.

Man lives not for himself alone,
In others' good he finds his own;
Life's worth in fellowship is known.
We, friends and comrades on life's way,
Gather within these walls to pray:
Bless thou our fellowship today.
—HENRY C. SHUTTLEWORTH.

STORY:

"AT THE TURN OF THE ROAD" [15]

THE RAIN poured uncompromisingly down and down, and the State Street crowd swarmed unceasingly on. The girl in the waterproof raglan and the small red turban looked from the holly-trimmed windows to the bundle-laden people swarming along outside them, and kept saying to herself that it was Christmas time, and that she surely was feeling very light-hearted and festive. But the water was dripping inside her collar, and her heart was taking on something of the sogginess of her feet. The feeling of desolation was creeping so overpoweringly upon her that she threw back her head and said to herself: "Some day I shall be famous; some day my pictures will be hung in the great galleries of the world, and then I shall look back to this, and say it was very funny." Usually that anticipation of future triumphs went a long way in the mitigation of present discomforts; but today, though she said the words with stern stoutness, the idea was without its charm. All about her were people—people—people, and she was the only one in the great throng to whom Christmas would mean nothing.

She went as far as the Library Building, and there something made her stop. She could go up to the reading room and find the paper from home; it would tell her how her friends—who were not ambitious—were spending Christmas. It would cheer her to see familiar names on the printed page, and convince her that somewhere in the world a Christmas was waiting, if the pictures of the future would but permit her to go and take it.

The big room was almost empty—Chicago had little time for the reading of newspapers on the day before Christmas. She walked down the long aisle toward the alcove where she knew the Des

Moines paper was to be found. A man was standing before it—a man past middle years—and he was reading intently. He looked up and, seeing the girl in the wet raglan and turban, said, "I have just finished," as he pushed the paper toward her. It was the paper she had read in other days—the paper which the people whom she loved might be reading even now. She forgot the brutally big Chicago—forgot even the pictures of the future. The red turban went down into the sheltering folds of the paper from home, and she bowed without reservation under a long-growing and all-powerful homesickness.

At last she sensed the presence of someone beside her, and looking up she saw the man who had given her the paper.

"Little girl," he said, "are you lonesome?—discouraged? What is it? Can't you go home for Christmas?"

The voice was a kind one, and it was a face which seemed to understand. It did not occur to her that he was a stranger. She nodded her head in answer to his question.

"Why can't you go home? They want you, don't they?"

She turned her tear-stained face to him in astonishment. "Want me!"—and the red turban went down again into the sheltering folds.

At last she looked up. "I'm ashamed to be such a baby; but—but it's the first one I ever spent away from home, and there's something awful about feeling lonesome at Christmas-time."

"And now," he asked, with gentle insistence, "will you tell me why it is you are not going home?"

She flushed, and then threw back her head. "It's for art. I am studying here. Like most of the art students, I haven't much money. I am living for the future—sacrificing for it. I cannot afford to go home for Christmas."

The stranger looked at her peculiarly—his lips smiling, his eyes sad. "And so," he said, "the world goes on making the same old mistakes, living over the same old tragedies."

She turned on him questioningly. "Don't you think it is right to sacrifice for my work? Don't you believe I will be glad sometime I lived for other things than the present?"

For a moment he did not answer; then he said abruptly: "If you will sit down here by the window, I will tell you a little story. Thirty years ago I was standing just where you are standing today. You have made up your mind to get fame; I had made up my mind to get

—54—

money. I grant you that yours is a nobler ambition, but that matters little. I had determined to do the things I believed I could do; and, like you, I was prepared to sacrifice. I did just what you are planning to do now—cut myself off from my friends. I am a rich man today— but—but somehow the world is a rather lonely place for me. I cannot hope to make you see it, but after years of isolation—consecration you may call it, if you like—one loses the capacity for friendship—for real friendship. Strange, isn't it? but it's very true. And some way, my little friend, the human heart was not made to feed upon gratified ambition. Shall I tell you why I am here today? I live in New York City now, but I came out to Chicago on business. I judge that your home is in Des Moines; mine was there, too, once—it was from Des Moines I started out to get rich. This afternoon, as I saw the bustle on the streets, I realized that it was the day before Christmas, and then it flashed upon me that I was very near the one place in the world that had ever been a home to me. I thought it would seem good to go back there—to see some old friends, and to have a good, old-fashioned Christmas. I determined to get hold of a Des Moines paper, and if I could find the name of any person I thought would really care to see me, I would go out there and spend Christmas. Well, I've looked the paper all over, and I'm going back to New York."

"Oh, don't do that," cried the girl, stretching out an impulsive hand to him; "their names didn't happen to be in today; they'll be glad to see you—I know they will."

He shook his head. "It's hopeless. I don't think I should even be glad to see them. I've lived beyond it. It's too late for me; but— I've determined to ask something of you."

They looked at one another steadily for a minute, and then he put his hand in his pocket and took out a roll of bills. "Oh," she gasped. "Oh, thank you—no."

"My little friend," he said, "it's just like this. I've gone over the path, and I want to steer you the other way. You'll paint your pictures all right, I'm sure of that—you have the look of success in your eyes; but I want you to hold on to the other things, too. I'm not a religious man, certainly not a superstitious one, but I can't help feeling that I was sent here to find you today. I want you to take this money and spend Christmas where a girl should spend it—at home. I'll eat my dinner on the dining car tomorrow, and when I sit down at a table all alone, I shall be almost contented if I can say to myself, 'That little art girl's out home with her friends now; she's having the right kind of Christmas.'"

He had pushed the bills toward her; she looked at them uncertainly, but when she turned to speak to him he was gone.

She looked from the window and saw that the rain had turned to old-fashioned snow. Just then electric lights flashed on in a store across the street, and there blazed through the dusk a holly-clad "Merry Christmas."

POEM: *"Stimulus of Friendship"* [16]

Because of your firm faith, I kept the track
  Whose sharp stones my strength had almost spent—
I could not meet your eyes, if I turned back,
    So on I went.

Because of your strong love, I held my path
  When battered, worn and bleeding in the fight—
How could I meet your true eyes, blazing wrath?
    So I kept right.

—AUTHOR UNKNOWN.

PRAYER:

O Thou Guide and Companion of the Way, we thank Thee that Thou hast created so many things for our enjoyment. We thank Thee for the joy of companionship. As we go about our daily tasks, touching the lives of others, grant that we may never make the mistake of cutting ourselves off from human contacts, but may we strive to become friends of all we meet. Forgive us if we have been unfriendly or unkind to anyone. Forbid that we should ever utter a mean word, or do a thoughtless act which would mar our friendships. Forbid that we should in any way bring shame or reproach upon our friends. Grant unto us the wisdom to sense the needs of our friends and increase our capacity for real friendships. May we go beyond our human contacts to a greater comradeship with Thee. In Jesus' name we pray. AMEN.

HYMN: *"Love Thyself Last,"* or
    "The Touch of Human Hands," "Blest Be the Tie,"
    "Christ of the Upward Way."

BENEDICTION:

Father, give Thy benediction and grant us Thy peace as we part. AMEN.

GROUP II

Christian Living

SERVICE VI: EACH IN HIS PLACE

AIM: To lead to a discovery of one's place in the world and the type of work which he is best able to do.

INSTRUMENTAL PRELUDE: *"Litany"* (SCHUBERT).

CALL TO WORSHIP:

> Worship the Lord in the beauty of holiness,
>   Bow down before Him, His glory proclaim;
> Gold of obedience, and incense of lowliness,
>   Kneel and adore Him—the Lord is His name.
>
> Low at His feet lay thy burden of carefulness,
>   High on His heart He will bear it for thee,
> Comfort thy sorrows, and answer thy prayerfulness,
>   Guiding thy steps as may best for thee be.
>   —JOHN S. B. MONSELL.

SCRIPTURE: Matthew 25: 14-29.

HYMN: *"O Son of Man, Thou Madest Known,"* or
    "Be Strong, We Are Not Here to Play."

STORY:

"ITS MISSION" [17]

THE STUDIO was far up on the top floor of a great building; and when one entered it, there was little to tell one of the greatness of the man who worked there. The floor was littered with bits of glass, putty, and lead. All seemed to be disorder and confusion.

Very early one morning a boy entered the studio bearing in his hands a basket containing bits of glass. Very carefully he laid them on the table, but as he turned his basket caught a tiny fragment of glass and swept it to the floor. He tried to find it; then the ringing of a bell caused him to leave the room, and the glass was forgotten.

It was only a piece of glass, so what did it matter? It had little beauty, for it was jagged and rough. It was small and lacking in color, so no one noticed it all through the day. It was kicked by the messenger; brushed aside by the maid; and, finally, several days later, found itself in a pile of rubbish, ready to be carried to the street.

Now the bit of glass had had dreams of greatness when it had been chosen by the master. It had dreams of some day being a part of a great window in a beautiful church. So, as it found itself being pushed farther and farther into the corner, it said to itself, "O dear, I had hoped to be of some use somewhere. How dreadful it will be to be thrown out into the street with old bottles and bits of glass. I am sure the master meant me for some good use, for he was so careful in choosing me. I wonder if there isn't any way by which I can be found. If someone comes this way, I shall prick. If the sunshine comes in the corner, I shall shine. But there seems to be nothing else that I can do; I will try, for I do not want to be thrown away."

So it glistened as best it could, but no one saw. It turned its sharp corners straight up, but no one came near.

After some days, the master came to the studio and began to work. He drew aside a homely curtain that was pulled across the rear of the room, and the sunshine streamed through a wonderful window upon which he was working. In the lower part of the window there were many, many little children, looking up and smiling. All about them were flowers. Above the children was the figure of a man, as yet incomplete.

With a happy smile, the artist seated himself before the picture. He looked long at the work he had already done. Then he began to put in the pieces of glass which he had laid on the table. There was a red piece that finished the robe of the man. Other bits of glass made his hand.

The little bit of glass in the corner heard him talking to himself as he worked. "This is to be my very best," he said. "So many, many months I have worked to make this window. I must tell to the world how much I love the Christ. It must be beautiful to show his beauty.

If I can only make it express what I feel, how glad I shall be." And he sang as he worked.

The days went by, and as friends stood beside the artist and talked to him, the bit of glass in the corner knew that the window was almost completed. And because it knew this, more and more plainly came the thought, "I was mistaken. There is no place for me in the window; I shall never be missed. I cannot help to show the beauty of the Christ to the world. There is no place for me in the plan of the artist."

Suddenly there was a commotion in the studio. The artist went from one place to another looking for something. The boy was sent for and questioned. Then he was sent to the factory to see if he could find what had been lost. The table was moved; the books were moved; the floor was carefully swept. And the glass heard the artist say: "I can't finish without it. It was such a wonderful piece, and I had spent so much time and thought on it. Where can it be? I just must have it to finish the window. I must have it. I must."

Then the bit of glass in the corner began to dream again: "Can it be I? Could I be an important part of the window? Will the picture be spoiled if I am not there? Did he make me carefully for a special place? Oh, I hope so! I hope some one will find me. All I can do is to shine. I will catch the beam of sunshine that is stealing across the floor, and perhaps someone will see me shine."

So the bit of glass did its best, and the sunshine helped it to sparkle and gleam.

There was a cry of delight, and the bit of glass was pulled from the rubbish pile where it had lain with the other useless things. It was laid in the hand of the master, and turned over and over to see if it had been harmed by its contact with common things. Then it was polished and carried to the window.

A placing of glass, a bit of leading, and lo! the small piece of glass which others had thought useless and not beautiful was the eye of the Christ in the window. The rough places found just their companion pieces, and the color gleamed in the light.

Carefully the artist put it into its place. Eagerly he watched to see what story it would tell. And when he stepped away and looked into the face of the Christ, the eye was full of tenderness, love, and compassion. It told to the world the love of the artist for the Christ.

And the bit of glass? Ah! it went out into the world, into the niche of a great and beautiful church. It was one of the smallest and most unattractive bits of glass in the whole window when left by itself; but when used in the way that the master meant it to be, it became the heart of the window.

To those who looked into the window when they were sad, it brought comfort; to those who were lonely, it brought a message of friendship; to the children, it told of the love of the Master. To all who looked into the window there came a message of love and beauty. The bit of glass had found its place—and was content.

LITANY OF WORK:

Leader: For the desire that we have to find our place in the life of the world,

Response: We praise Thee, O God.

Leader: For the opportunity of becoming a useful member of society,

Response: We thank Thee, O God.

Leader: For the chance of working at some worth-while task,

Response: We give Thee Thanks, O God.

Leader: For the dignity and honor of labor, and the joy that comes from reaching a worthy goal,

Response: We thank Thee, O God.

Leader: For the chance to contribute through work to the happiness of those we love,

Response: We praise Thee, O God.

Leader: For the privilege of sharing in Thy purpose for us by accepting our share of the world's work,

Response: We humbly thank Thee, O God.

Leader: Grant that we may make service the motive of our life,

Response: In Jesus' name, we pray. AMEN.

HYMN: *"O Master Workman of the Race."*

BENEDICTION:

O Merciful Father, we beseech Thee, dismiss us in Thy favor, and may we go forth to find useful work according to Thy purpose for our lives. AMEN.

GROUP II

Christian Living

SERVICE VII: A CONSECRATED VESSEL

AIM: To awaken a desire to make of oneself a consecrated vessel which may be used in the cause of Christ in the world.

INSTRUMENTAL PRELUDE: *"Song without Words"* (MENDELSSOHN).

CALL TO WORSHIP (in unison):

O Lord our God, how excellent is thy name in all the earth! who hast set thy glory above the heavens. Out of the mouth of babes and sucklings hast thou ordained strength because of thine enemies, that thou mightest still the enemy and the avenger. When I consider thy heavens, the work of thy fingers, the moon and the stars, which thou hast ordained; what is man, that thou art mindful of him? and the son of man, that thou visitest him? For thou hast made him a little lower than the angels, and hast crowned him with glory and honor. Thou madest him to have dominion over the works of thy hands; thou hast put all things under his feet: all sheep and oxen, yea, all the beasts of the field; the fowl of the air, and the fish of the sea, and whatsoever passeth through the paths of the seas. O Lord our Lord, how excellent is thy name in all the earth! [18]

PRAYER HYMN: *"Draw Thou My Soul, O Christ"*
Draw Thou my soul, O Christ,
  Closer to Thine;
Breathe into every wish
  Thy will divine!
Raise my low self above,
Won by Thy deathless love;

Ever, O Christ, through mine
Let Thy life shine.

Lead forth my soul, O Christ,
One with Thine own,
Joyful to follow Thee
Through paths unknown!
In Thee my strength renew;
Give me my work to do!
Through me Thy truth be shown,
Thy love made known.
—LUCY LARCOM.

RESPONSIVE READING:

Leader: Wherewith shall a young man cleanse his way? by taking
heed thereto according to thy word.

Response (to be sung):

O Jesus, I have promised
To serve Thee to the end;
Be Thou forever near me,
My Master and my friend;
I shall not fear the battle
If Thou art by my side,
Nor wander from the pathway
If Thou wilt be my guide.

Leader: With my whole heart have I sought thee: O let me not wander
from thy commandments.

Response:

O let me feel Thee near me!
The world is ever near;
I see the sights that dazzle,
The tempting sounds I hear;
My foes are ever near me,
Around me and within;
But, Jesus, draw Thou nearer,
And shield my soul from sin.

Leader: Thy word have I hid in mine heart, that I might not sin
against thee.[19]

Response:

> O let me hear Thee speaking
> In accents clear and still,
> Above the storms and passion,
> The murmurs of self-will:
> O speak to reassure me,
> To hasten or control;
> O speak and make me listen,
> Thou guardian of my soul.
> —JOHN E. BODE.

PRAYER (in unison):

Almighty God, unto whom all hearts are open, all desires known, and from whom no secrets are hid: cleanse the thoughts of our hearts by the inspiration of Thy Holy Spirit: that we may perfectly love Thee and worthily magnify Thy holy name, through Jesus Christ our Lord. AMEN.[20]

STORY:

"THE HANDFUL OF CLAY" [21]

THERE was a handful of clay in the bank of a river. It was only common clay, coarse and heavy; but it had high thoughts of its own value, and wonderful dreams of the great place which it was to fill in the world when the time came for its virtues to be discovered.

Overhead, in the spring sunshine, the trees whispered together of the glory which descended upon them when the delicate blossoms and leaves began to expand, and the forest glowed with fair, clear colors, as if the dust of thousands of rubies and emeralds were hanging, in soft clouds, above the earth.

The flowers, surprised with the joy of beauty, bent their heads to one another, as the wind caressed them, and said: "Sisters, how lovely you have become. You make the day bright."

The river, glad of new strength and rejoicing in the unison of all its waters, murmured to the shores in music, telling of its release from icy fetters, its swift flight from the snow-clad mountains, and the mighty work to which it was hurrying—the wheels of many mills to be turned, and great ships to be floated to the sea.

Waiting blindly in its bed, the clay comforted itself with lofty hopes. "My time will come," it said. "I was not made to be hidden forever. Glory and beauty and honor are coming to me in due season."

One day the clay felt itself taken from the place where it had waited so long. A flat blade of iron passed beneath it, lifted it, tossed it into a cart with other lumps of clay, and it was carried far away, as it seemed, over a rough and stony road. But it was not afraid, nor discouraged, for it said to itself: "This is necessary. The path to glory is always rugged. Now I am on my way to play a great part in the world."

But the hard journey was nothing compared with the tribulation and distress that came after it. The clay was put into a trough and mixed and beaten and stirred and trampled. It seemed almost unbearable. But there was consolation in the thought that something very fine and noble was certainly coming out of all this trouble. The clay felt sure that, if it could only wait long enough, a wonderful reward was in store for it.

Then it was put upon a swiftly turning wheel, and whirled around until it seemed as if it must fly into a thousand pieces. A strange power pressed and molded it as it revolved, and through all the dizziness and pain the clay felt that it was taking a new form.

Then an unknown hand put it into an oven and fires were kindled about it—fierce and penetrating, hotter than all the heats of summer that had ever brooded upon the bank of the river. But through it all the clay held itself together and endured its trials, in the confidence of a great future. "Surely," it thought, "I am intended for something very splendid, since such pains are taken with me. Perhaps I am fashioned for the ornament of a temple, or a precious vase for the table of a king."

At last the baking was finished. The clay was taken from the furnace and set down upon a board in the cool air, under the blue sky. The tribulation was passed. The reward was at hand.

Close beside the board there was a pool of water, not very deep, not very clear, but calm enough to reflect with impartial truth every image that fell upon it. There, for the first time, as it was lifted from the board, the clay saw its new shape, the reward of all its patience and pain, the consummation of its hopes—a common flowerpot, straight and stiff, red and ugly. And then it felt that it was not destined for a king's mansion, nor for a palace of art, because it was made without glory or beauty or honor; and it murmured against the unknown maker, saying, "Why hast thou made me thus?"

Many days it passed in sullen discontent. Then it was filled with earth, and something rough and brown and dead-looking was thrust into the middle of the earth and covered over. The clay rebelled at this new disgrace. "This is the worst of all that has happened to me, to be filled with dirt and rubbish. Surely I am a failure."

But presently it was set in a greenhouse, where the sunlight fell warm upon it, water was sprinkled over it, and day by day, as it waited, a change began to come to it. Something was stirring within it—a new hope. Still it was ignorant, not knowing what the new hope meant.

One day the clay was lifted again from its place and carried into a great church. Its dream was coming true, after all. It had a fine part to play in the world. Still it could not understand. So it whispered to another vessel of clay, like itself, close beside it, "Why have they set me here? Why do all the people look toward us?"

And the other vessel answered, "Do you not know? You are carrying a royal scepter of lilies. Their petals are white as snow, and the heart of them is like pure gold. The people look this way because the flower is the most wonderful in the world. And the root of it is in your heart."

Then the clay was content, and silently thanked its maker, because, though an earthen vessel, it held so great a treasure.

POEM:
> "Build thee more stately mansions, O my soul,
> As the swift seasons roll!
> Leave thy low-vaulted past!
> Let each new temple, nobler than the last,
> Shut thee from heaven with a dome more vast,
> Till thou at length art free,
> Leaving thine outgrown shell by life's unresting sea." [23]
> —OLIVER WENDELL HOLMES.

PRAYER:

O God, we lift our hearts in thanksgiving to Thee for all Thy blessings. We praise Thee for Thy revealed truth which has been a lamp unto our feet and a light unto our path. We thank Thee for every good impulse which comes from Thee. Reveal unto us the things in our lives which keep us from being fit instruments for Thy use. We would consecrate every faculty of mind and body to Thy service. Take away from us any selfishness, lack of purpose, or low ideals which would keep us from following Thee completely. Forgive us for the times when we have failed to heed Thy promptings. Awaken within us holy desires, inspire us with new visions, and endow us with a new enthusiasm as we strive to follow the example of Jesus. Reveal unto us the things which we may do to further Thy cause in the world. In Jesus' name we pray. AMEN.

HYMN: *"Lord, Speak to Me, That I May Speak"*

> Lord, speak to me, that I may speak
>   In living echoes of Thy tone;
> As Thou hast sought, so let me seek
>   Thine erring children lost and lone.
>
> O teach me, Lord, that I may teach
>   The precious things Thou dost impart;
> And wing my words, that they may reach
>   The hidden depths of many a heart.
>
> O fill me with Thy fullness, Lord,
>   Until my very heart o'erflow
> In kindling thought and glowing word,
>   Thy love to tell, Thy praise to show.
>
> O use me, Lord, use even me,
>   Just as Thou wilt, and when, and where;
> Until Thy blessed face I see,
>   Thy rest, Thy joy, Thy glory share. Amen.
>   —FRANCES R. HAVERGAL.

BENEDICTION:

The Lord bless you and keep you; the Lord lift His countenance upon you, and give you peace; the Lord make His face to shine upon you, and be gracious unto you. AMEN.

GROUP II

Christian Living

SERVICE VIII: WITHOUT COUNTING THE COST

AIM: To challenge the group to choose the right regardless of the decisions of the crowd.

INSTRUMENTAL PRELUDE: *"Pilgrim's Chorus"* from Tannhauser
(WAGNER).

CALL TO WORSHIP:

Leader:
> Enter into His gates with thanksgiving,
> And into His courts with praise.

Response:
> I was glad when they said unto me,
> Let us go into the house of the Lord.

Hymn Response (to be sung):
> The Lord is in His holy temple,
> The Lord is in His holy temple,
> Let all the earth keep silence,
> Let all the earth keep silence,
> Keep silence before Him. AMEN.

HYMN: *"March On, O Soul, with Strength,"* or
"Stand Up, Stand Up for Jesus."

SCRIPTURE:

He that dwelleth in the secret place of the Most High shall abide under the shadow of the Almighty. I will say of the Lord, He is my refuge and my fortress: my God; in him will I trust. Surely he shall deliver thee from the snare of the fowler, and from the noisome pestilence. He shall cover thee with his feathers, and under his wings shalt thou trust: his truth shall be thy shield and buckler. Thou shalt not be afraid for the terror by night; nor for the arrow that flieth by day. Nor for the pestilence that walketh in darkness; nor for the destruction that wasteth at noonday. The Lord is my light and my salvation; whom shall I fear? The Lord is the strength of my life; of whom shall I be afraid?[23]

PRAYER:

Almighty Father, we lift our hearts to Thee. With strange rites and beside crude altars many have sought Thy presence. Hear us as we strive to enter into fellowship with Thee. We need a peace far deeper than the world can give; we need Thy pardoning power in our lives. Purge us of all sins which we have committed. Forgive us for the promptings which we have failed to obey; for the acts of kindness which we have failed to do. May we go forth in newness of life to serve Thee. In the name of Jesus, we pray. AMEN.

STORY:

"FORTY GOOD SOLDIERS FOR CHRIST"

AFTER HIS conquest Caesar returned to Rome, leaving some of his legions to hold the conquered territory. The army thus left behind spent a long winter encamped in a cold northern province. During these months one of the early Christian missionaries found his way to the camp of Roman soldiers. He was cordially received and spent several months with them, teaching them about Christ and his way of living.

A number of Roman soldiers came to believe in the true God and were given Christian baptism. Among them were forty of the bravest soldiers in the camp. They were the pick of the legion—the favorites of the old Roman general who was in charge of them. They were his best soldiers, as well as his friends, and he loved them with a great love.

In the meantime Caesar had grown more ambitious. He was so sure of his power over his soldiers that he proclaimed himself the god of the Roman army and sent orders that the soldiers should worship him. In fact, the edict had gone throughout the Roman empire that all should worship the Emperor. Symbols were set up everywhere and all were commanded to bow down to them as to the Emperor.

This order to worship Caesar came to the general in charge of the camp in Gaul. He called before him the faithful legions and read to them the proclamation that Caesar is God and the edict that all must worship him. He ordered a huge altar erected to Caesar, and sent commands to the captains of the host to have the soldiers pass in single file before the altar and place thereon a portion of incense as a symbol of their worship of Caesar.

All day long the Roman soldiers marched by the great altar, and at the close of the day every man had placed incense on the altar except the forty good soldiers. They refused to worship any except the true God. The general called them before him and begged them to recant, but to no avail. He decided to give them another chance; but if they failed, they would be sentenced to death by exposure on the frozen lake nearby.

As the evening drew near there was a stillness over the entire legion. Every one was asking, "What will the Christians do?" Again they were marched by Caesar's altar, but not a man laid incense on it. True to his word, the general stripped them of their armor, lined them up on the shore, and gave the order to march out across the frozen lake. With unfaltering courage, with radiant faces, and with firm steps the valiant soldiers marched away singing:

> "Forty good soldiers for Christ are we,
>   And we will not give up our God;
>   O Christ, we claim for Thee the victory,
>   And ask from Thee the crown."

The general stood by the camp fire near the shore, gazing intently as they marched away. Long after they had passed out of sight he listened to their song until the fire became nothing but red embers. Their voices grew fainter and fainter. As the night wore on he could barely hear from the distance the challenging words, "Forty good soldiers for Christ are we." He paced the shore in agony, wondering how many of them were still alive. They were his best soldiers! How he would miss them!

In the darkness he stood straining his eyes to catch a glimpse of them. At last he fancied that he saw something—yes, someone was coming from the lake! And he was not singing! Who could it be? As he drew nearer the general saw, groveling up the bank, one of the forty soldiers. He was making his way to the altar cautiously, as though he wanted to keep himself hidden from all human eyes. He bowed and placed his incense upon the altar and slipped away to his tent.

With a cry the general threw off his helmet and his coat of mail, ran down the shore, out upon the frozen lake, to join the band of Christians, singing as he went. Once more there rang out the glorious words of victory:

> "Forty good soldiers for Christ are we,
> And we will not give up our God;
> O Christ, we claim for Thee the victory,
> And we ask from Thee the crown."

Litany of Praise:

Leader: For that noble throng of saints of all ages and all lands who have stood steadfastly for the right against the wrong,

Response: We praise Thee, O God.

Leader: For the heritage which these great servants of Thine have passed on to us,

Response: We praise Thee, O God.

Leader: For the example of those who were willing to suffer that Thy truth may be preserved.

Response: We praise Thee, O God.

Leader: For the courage of those who were indifferent to public opinion,

Response: We praise Thee, O God.

Leader: Grant that we may endure hardness as a good soldier of Jesus Christ.

Response: Hear our prayer, O God.

Leader: Remove from us all fear, all cowardice, all uncertainty, and give unto us that perfect love which casteth out fear.

Response: Hear our prayer, O God.

Leader: Strengthened by Thy spirit, may we strive to follow in the steps of those great heroes of the past who counted not their own lives dear unto them.

Response: Hear our prayer, O God.

Leader: Grant unto us the high gift of courage that we may follow daily the example of the Master,

Response: In whose name we pray. Amen.

HYMN: *"God's Trumpet Wakes the Slumbering World."*

BENEDICTION:

Our Father, dismiss us in Thy favor, and may we go forth to follow the right regardless of the decisions of others.

GROUP II

Christian Living

SERVICE IX: THE UPWARD CLIMB

AIM: To uphold in the thinking of the group the possibilities for growth and development regardless of the handicaps.

INSTRUMENTAL PRELUDE: *Larghetto from Sonata in D* (HANDEL).

CALL TO WORSHIP:

Thus saith the high and lofty one, that inhabiteth eternity, whose name is Holy: I dwell in the high and holy place, with him also that is of a contrite and humble spirit. Seek ye the Lord while he may be found; Call ye upon him while he is near: Let the wicked forsake his way, and the unrighteous man his thoughts; and let him return unto the Lord, and he will have mercy upon him; And to our God, for he will abundantly pardon.

HYMN: *"Dear Master, in Whose Life I See,"* or *"Purer Yet and Purer."*

RESPONSIVE READING: *"Old Testament Beatitudes."*

Leader: Blessed is the man whose strength is in God: in whose hearts are the ways of them.

Response: Teach me thy way, O Lord: I will walk in thy truth.

Leader: Blessed are they that dwell in thy house, they will be still praising thee.

Response: Blessed are the upright in the way, who walk in the way of the Lord.

Leader: Blessed are they that keep his testimonies; that seek him with the whole heart.

Response: Blessed is the man that delighteth greatly in his commandments.

"New Testament Beatitudes"

Leader: Blessed are the poor in spirit: for theirs is the kingdom of heaven.

Response: Help us to obtain this blessing.

Leader: Blessed are the meek: for they shall inherit the earth.

Response: O God, enable us to obtain this blessing.

Leader: Blessed are they that hunger and thirst after righteousness: for they shall be filled.

Response: Lord, be gracious unto us, and help us to obtain this blessing.

Leader: Blessed are the pure in heart: for they shall see God.

Response: Grant us thy Holy Spirit, O God, and enable us to obtain all these blessings, through Jesus Christ our Lord.

SCRIPTURE RESPONSE:

> Thy word have I hid in my heart,
> That I might not sin against thee.
> Blessed art thou, O Lord my God:
> Teach me thy statutes.

OFFERTORY:

Leader: Let every man give according as he hath purposed in his heart: not grudgingly or of necessity; for God loveth a cheerful giver.

Response (to be sung):

> Bless thou the gifts our hands have brought;
> Bless thou the work our hearts have planned;
> Ours is the faith, the will, the thought;
> The rest, O God, is in thy hand.

STORY:

"THE ST. JOHN'S FUND" [24]

WHEN the sexton of St. John's Church entered the vestibule he was instinctively aware that in some way the church was not just as he had left it the night before. When he turned his eyes to the chancel window he discovered at once wherein the difference lay. Instead of the enraptured face of St. John the Divine, which had shone there yesterday, there was now a great jagged opening, and the deep blue background of Judean sky was cracked and shattered to the leads.

One moment the sexton stood amazed and horrified; the next he turned and rushed out to seek the rector.

A ragged urchin stood on the opposite sidewalk, behind the trunk of a great tree, watching his chance; and the moment the sexton's face was turned away from him he darted across the pavement, up the steps, and into the church. Once inside, he looked for an instant toward the radiant window and the headless St. John; then, white-faced and terror-stricken, turned and fled.

Five minutes later, the Rev. Mr. Pancoast, rector of the church, stood gazing on the wrecked window in silence. The St. John had been his pride, his inspiration. Many a time he had felt the power of its presence as he ministered at the altar. And now it was gone—blotted out—ruthlessly, wickedly destroyed.

He strode down the aisle and up to the chancel rail with the rising fires of anger and indignation burning in his breast. But under the broken bits of glass he discovered a ball—a boy's baseball, old, ragged, dirty. As he picked it up and looked at it, the fire went out of his eyes, the angry lines left his face, and he turned to the sexton and said: "It was a boy's carelessness; we must not judge too harshly."

But his vestry did not agree with him. "It's a piece of sacrilege! It's outrageous, simply outrageous!"

"But," said the rector calmly, "I believe that it was an accident, and the one who did it will have the manhood to come and acknowledge his fault and offer reparation."

He had hardly finished speaking when the housemaid entered the room and handed him a soiled envelope. "A boy came to the door with it, sir, and ran away as soon as ever I got my hand on it."

When the rector tore open the envelope a ten-cent silver piece rolled out of it and fell to the floor. In the envelope was a letter, as follows:

"Mr. Pankose i brok the winder i nokt the head offen him with a bas ball i guess i orto go to jale fer it. But ile pay for it if youse giff me time ile pay it all if youse giff me time and dont airest me. hears a dime tords it now and ile pay more in a weak."

"I believe that boy will do as he says!" declared the rector. He took the dime and put it in an envelope, across the back of which he wrote: "The St. John's Fund."

It was ten days before the confessed culprit was again heard from. This time his letter contained only a five-cent piece. He wrote: "Hears a nikel for the winder i caint pay no more this time caus my muthers too sick if youse only giff me time ile pay it al shure." After that a nickel came each week with much regularity.

Winter came and went. A celebrated artist had made a new St. John for the broken window. The people were to see it for the first time on Easter Sunday morning. But it chanced that on the Saturday before Easter the doors of the church were opened to admit a funeral. The rector of the church, out of the goodness of his heart, had offered to read the services of the church over some poor, wasted bit of clay. On the face of the woman as she lay before the chancel was written the story of another life ground out under the pitiless heel of poverty. The one standing near by was the boy who had darted into the church that morning six months before to gaze in terror for a moment on the wreck his careless hands had wrought.

At the close of the service the boy glanced up at the chancel window where the benignant and beautiful face of the new St. John seemed to gaze upon him with a sympathy and affection which in all his pinched and miserable life he had never seen in any other face save that one which was now shut out forever from his sight.

Four weeks went by with no contribution to the fund. But one day a letter came, postmarked Chicago, enclosing twenty-five cents, saying: "I'm wurkin now, I'm cash boy in a store. My unkel got me the place. My muther she died. Mr. Pankose i wisht i could tel you now but i caint but youse been awful good to me."

After that the money came at regular intervals. At one time he gave as an excuse for not sending a larger instalment the fact that he was attending a night school. His spelling and handwriting began to show a marked improvement. Later he wrote that he had a responsible position in a shoe department.

On his fourteenth birthday he sent a crisp new dollar bill to be added to the St. John's Fund. He wrote that he was still attending night school, and was saving his money to take lessons from a private tutor.

On his fifteenth birthday he sent five dollars, and all that year he sent the same amount regularly each month. He had entered high school and hoped to graduate with his class.

On his sixteenth birthday he sent ten dollars, and when it was handed to the treasurer he replied: "For pity's sake! Is there no way to stop it? Have we got to take it whether or no? We've got enough now, with the interest, to pay for the window. It ought to be stopped."

So they decided to insert a notice in one of the Chicago daily papers to the effect that no more money was needed for the window of St. John's Church. The reply came that the writer deeply appreciated their kindness and that he hoped some day to make open confession for his fault. There was no signature, no address. At the next meeting of the vestry it was voted to allow the St. John's Fund to remain intact until it could be put to a use as noble as the spirit which had led to its foundation.

The years came and went. All the members of the vestry passed on except the treasurer. The rector after forty years of service had resigned. Poor in purse he still was, but rich in spirit and in the love of his parishioners. A new rector had been called—a man from the far west. No one in the parish knew him, but the bishop had recommended him most highly. His ministry was to begin, and that of the old rector was to end, on Easter Sunday.

The church had never been so beautiful as it was on that Sunday. The new rector brought a message which carried him at once to the heart of his people. When the sermon was ended, he left the pulpit and came out in front of the chancel rail. For a moment he stood, looking silently over the throng of people, as if the power of speech had suddenly left him. When he began he halted and stumbled, and it was apparent that he was laboring under a severe mental strain.

"I cannot continue another hour as your pastor until I have confessed to you an offense committed by me against this church and this people many years ago. To you, it may seem trivial, but it has lain on my conscience since boyhood. When I was a lad I lived in this city. One night, in a freak of boyhood recklessness, I hurled my ball through the chancel window of this church. For the material damage I have made such reparation as I could, but I did not have the courage to confess my fault. God has brought me to the point where I can no longer keep silent and remain a minister of Christ. I confess my fault to you now, and am ready to meet your condemnation. I can hardly hope for your forgiveness."

He paused, as if trying to master some great emotion. The people in the pews were thunderstruck. "I wish to add one word more. In my boyhood I lived with my invalid mother in direst poverty. She died six months after I broke the window. In the midst of my distress, like a vision of light, came the rector of this church. We were not of this flock, yet he comforted me." He turned to the old rector and said: "I can only pray that your mantle may fall on me, and that this people may remember in gratitude your forty years of love and devotion to them."

The treasurer arose, advanced to the chancel steps and faced the people: "I may be breaking a rule of this church by speaking now, but I want to say that the boy who broke that window paid for it thirty years ago. The money has been invested and stands today on our books at more than thirty-seven thousand dollars. At a meeting last evening it was voted that this fund should be used for the maintenance and comfort of the late rector."

The treasurer went back to his pew. As the new rector looked over the congregation, every face was radiant with sympathy and joy. The magnificent strains of "Old Hundred" rolled out from the organ, and never before did the walls of the old church ring with melody that came so straight from hearts to lips, as they did while the people sang "Praise God" on the beautiful Easter morning.

POEM: *"I Will Follow the Upward Road"* [25]

I will follow the upward road today,
    I will keep my face to the light.
I will keep high thoughts as I go my way,
    I will do what I know is right.
I will look for flowers by the side of the road,
    I will laugh and love and be strong.
I will try to lighten another's load
    This day as I fare along.

—MARY S. EDGAR.

PRAYER:

O Thou, who art the strength of our life, we thank Thee for the adventure of living and all the joys it brings. We bless Thee for every impulse to do good; for all the strivings to follow the upward way; for the discipline of hard work. Grant unto us the courage to follow truth unafraid, and the strength to resist temptations. Help us to control ourselves in such a way as to develop our capacities to the highest. May we determine to live according to the Light that has come from Thee. Grant unto us the wisdom to discern the true from the false, the good from the evil, and may no unworthy purpose draw us aside; but as we travel along the road, may we find new ways of serving Thee. We bring this prayer in the name of Him who taught us the Way of Life. Amen.

HYMN: *"Christ of the Upward Way,"* or *"I Would Be True."*

BENEDICTION:

May the peace of God rule in your hearts, and the word of Christ dwell in you richly in all wisdom. AMEN.

GROUP III

Living Together as Brothers

SERVICE X: COLOR BLIND

AIM: To create a desire to rid one's self of racial prejudice.

INSTRUMENTAL PRELUDE: "Largo," from Dvorak's "New World Symphony."

CALL TO WORSHIP:

One is your Father, who is in heaven;
And all ye are brethren.
God hath made of one blood all nations of men to dwell on
all the face of the earth;
Therefore all things whatsoever ye would that men should
do to you, do ye even so to them.
O come, let us worship; let us kneel before the Lord, our
maker.

SPIRITUAL: *"Lord, I Want to Be a Christian."* [26]

RESPONSIVE READING:

Leader: Lord, who shall abide in Thy tabernacle? Who shall dwell
in Thy holy hill?

Response: He that walketh uprightly, and worketh righteousness,
And speaketh the truth in his heart.

Leader: They shall come from the east, and from the west, and from
the north, and from the south, And shall sit down in the kingdom of God.

Response: For whosoever shall do the will of my Father which is in
heaven, the same is my brother, and sister, and mother.

Leader: Hereby shall all men know that we are His disciples, because we have love one to another;

Response: For if we love not men whom we have seen, how can we love God whom we have not seen?[27]

HYMN: *"Where Cross the Crowded Ways of Life."*

STORY:

"THE SECRET OF ONE MAN'S POWER" [28]

ROLAND HAYES has recently completed the most successful and triumphant year of his artistic career. Being eager to know the reason for his success, I sought an interview with him. When I knocked at the door of his hotel room I found him busy telephoning, but he cheerfully bade me enter. He waved his hand in friendly greeting and I felt immediately the warm, courteous, engaging atmosphere that his very presence creates.

I noticed that he had just finished breakfast in his room, for the dishes were still there. So I began the conversation by remarking that I was exceedingly sorry for a condition in our social order that made it necessary for a colored man of his sensitive nature to stay away from public dining-rooms and to enter hotels by side doors. "There is nothing that you or any white man can do to alter that," said Mr. Hayes. "That is a job for me and my people. I am trying to live every moment with such consciousness of the Divine Presence and with no trace of bitterness in my heart that that condition of racial prejudice shall disappear. And I am trying to influence my people to do likewise."

He paused and looked about the room and smiled as he resumed: "I am perfectly happy here by myself, and nobody in all the world can hurt me except myself." Then he told of a wonderful teacher who had warned him that as a black artist he would suffer many things if he allowed the barbs to get inside. "But always remember that if your heart is right and your spirit divinely disciplined, nobody in all the world can hurt you."

I then asked him if he had certain hours of communion and spiritual preparation for his concerts. He surprised me by saying that he did not. "Years ago I had certain hours, but now every breath I draw and every moment of the day is a communion with God." Then he asked if I would like to know how he captures his audience during his first minute on the stage. I was eager to know. "I stand there perfectly quiet with my hands clasped before me and pray—that Roland Hayes may be blotted entirely out of the picture—that the people sitting there may feel only the Spirit of God flowing through melody and rhythm—that racial prejudice may be forgotten. The audience instinctively feels what is happening as I commune with my Father—and I capture them that moment and never let them go until I am done."

The radiance and joy that emanated from this quiet-spoken little man was a thing that electrified the whole room. "What a time I have had this winter!" he said. "I have given up my expensive managers and the high-priced tickets they used to insist upon. Now I have no manager and I am free to insist that the prices be kept low so that the poor who long for my songs may come and hear them. The color line disappears—rich and poor, high and low, forget the barriers that ordinarily divide them, and we all become sons and daughters of a common Father, hushed and quieted by the haunting power of the message of melody and rhythm and song."

Then he told a very interesting story—only typical of what is happening to him constantly. In a town in New Jersey a Southern family decided to attend one of his concerts in order to show the fifteen-year-old son "what a horrible mess a 'nigger' makes out of life when he thinks he possesses talents that should be possessed only by white people." The parents had filled this lad with their prejudices and he came in that spirit. Mr Hayes with his usual technique blotted himself out of the picture, and the beauty of God shone through. The atmosphere, now of harmony and peace, now of pathos and sadness, was not marred by the ego of the artist breaking through. After the concert, this young man sought out his black brother and, throwing his arms about his neck, confessed that Mr. Hayes had done in two hours what all the books and orators in the world never could have accomplished. His lifelong prejudice was gone. "And now every time I see him," said Mr. Hayes, "he assures me that he is devoting his life to the cause of eradicating some of the prejudice in others similar to that his parents had fostered in him through the years."

Then he related a most remarkable incident: "A few years ago I gave a concert before a large and enthusiastic audience down in Alabama. The next day I journeyed to the old plantation where my mother had been a slave. The old master and his wife were still alive, but what a change the years had wrought! The affluence of the old days was gone. The plantation itself had gone to ruin and had been sold for debt. The old gentleman and his wife were barely existing in a little shanty. I introduced myself and asked them if they remembered my mother. Yes, of course they did—very well indeed. She was one of the dear souls they could never forget. They had called her 'Pony.' She was too much beloved to be allowed to live in the slave quarters, so she lived in the big house as a servant."

Mr. Hayes said that as he looked round about at the signs of poverty he could imagine the thoughts that were running through the old couple's mind—the contrast between the good old days, when Pony had been a slave and they had been wealthy, and their present poverty with Pony's son, one of the world's famous artists, standing before them. He wanted desperately to help them, but wondered whether their Southern pride would permit it.

Would this proud old couple accept his help? He used the familiar spiritual technique of the concert stage and obliterated himself. "Is there anything that Pony's son could do to help?" he finally asked. "Yes, I suppose so," came the answer. "I reached into my pocket and pulled out a check," said Mr. Hayes. "It was a large one —the returns from several of my largest concerts. The old lady was ill and was lying on the bed. I walked over and laid it on her chest. She picked it up and, seeing the size of it, suddenly realized that it meant getting the old plantation back and ending their days in peace. She threw open her arms, into which the aged master and I both fell. In a moment we had our arms about each other—just three of God's children, with no dividing color line."

POEM:

> I am not selfish now about the God I own,
>   I do not want a little God who can compress
> His goodness into bounds of just one land alone,
>   Who has a list preferred when he would bless
> His children—oh, the God I know
>   Is color blind; if yellow, red or black, or white,

He never notices the skin.
His blessings flow to give a light
To every race that stumbles through the night
To reach a remedy for sin.

—D. C. Bickers.

Prayer:

Lord Jesus, the reach of Thy love includes the whole world. Forgive our pettiness and prejudices. May others find it easier to draw near to Thee because of us. As Thou didst give Thyself without measure, may we, too, esteem others better than ourselves and serve in lowliness of mind. Forgive us every social condition that degrades humanity and is tolerated by us. Open our eyes to our world responsibility that we may do our full part in Thy name. Amen.[29]

Poem:

How many of us ever stop to think
Of music as a wondrous magic link
With God; taking sometimes the place of prayer,
When words have failed us 'neath the weight of care?
Music, that knows no country, race or creed;
But gives to each according to his need?

—Anonymous.

Hymn: *"These Things Shall Be: A Loftier Race"*

These things shall be a loftier race
    Than e'er the world hath known, shall rise
With flame of freedom in their souls,
    And light of knowledge in their eyes.

They shall be gentle, brave, and strong
    To spill no drop of blood, but dare
All that may plant man's lordship firm
    On earth, and fire, and sea, and air.

Nation with nation, land with land,
    Unarmed shall live as comrades free;
In every heart and brain shall throb
    The pulse of one fraternity.

New arts shall bloom of loftier mold,
And mightier music thrill the skies,
And every life shall be a song,
When all the earth is paradise.
—JOHN ADDINGTON SYMONDS.

BENEDICTION:

May the God of peace be with you all, both now and forevermore. AMEN.

GROUP III

Living Together as Brothers

SERVICE XI: A ROAD IS BUILT

AIM: To lead the group to consider the importance of a true spirit of brotherhood which will lead to kindness and good will.

INSTRUMENTAL PRELUDE: Hymn Tune: *"Palestrina."*

CALL TO WORSHIP:

> Great God of nations, now to Thee
> Our hymn of gratitude we raise;
> With humble heart and bending knee
> We offer Thee our song of praise.

> Great God, preserve us in Thy fear;
> In danger still our guardian be:
> O spread Thy truth's bright precepts here;
> Let all the people worship Thee.

HYMN: *"God Send Us Men Whose Aim 'Twill Be,"* or
"If I Can Stop One Heart from Breaking."

RESPONSIVE READING:

Leader: There is one God and Father of all,
Who is above all, and through all, and in you all.

Response: Behold what manner of love the Father hath bestowed upon us,
That we should be called the sons of God.

Leader: For I say, through the grace given unto me, to every man that is among you, not to think of himself more highly than he ought to think;

Response: But to think soberly, according as God hath dealt to every man the measure of faith.

Leader: For as we have many members in one body, and all members have not the same office:

Response: So we, being many, are one body in Christ, and every one members one of another.

Leader: Be kindly affectioned one to another with brotherly love; in honor preferring one another.

Response: Rejoice with them that do rejoice, and weep with them that weep. Be of the same mind one toward another.

Leader: Mind not high things, but condescend to men of low estate. Be not wise in your own conceits. Be not overcome of evil, but overcome evil with good.

Response: For with what judgment ye judge, ye shall be judged: and with what measure ye mete, it shall be measured unto you.[30]

Prayer (in unison):

> To Thee, Eternal Soul, be praise!
> Who from of old to our own days,
> Through souls of saints and prophets, Lord,
> Hath sent Thy light, Thy love, Thy word.
> We thank Thee for each mighty one
> Through whom Thy living light hath shone;
> And for each humble soul and sweet
> That lights to heaven our wandering feet.
>
> —RICHARD W. GILDER.

STORY:

"A ROAD IS BUILT" [31]

ROBERT LOUIS STEVENSON's father and grandfather were lighthouse engineers, but his health was too delicate for him to follow the same calling. The hours which he desired to spend out of doors and in play had to be spent in bed, but these hours were enlivened by his vivid imagination. As a lad he lived in a fairyland world with fairies and goblins as playmates and with tin soldiers to carry out his commands. Sometimes he sailed away to far-off seas where he engaged in many thrilling adventures and daring exploits. His mother urged him to write these stories, and in this way his career as a writer began very early in life.

Stevenson was seldom free from pain, yet he had a gayety and courage which had scarcely been equaled. From being a frail child he grew to be a man with very poor health, but this handicap did not keep him from writing cheerful books. One critic said that his books were far too cheerful; that he could not have known suffering, for he was so optimistic in his writings. Stevenson considered this the finest compliment that he ever received, for much of his writing was done when his body was racked with pain.

Later in life Stevenson decided to search until he found a place where he could have better health. After trying several countries, he settled on one of the Samoan Islands. Some of his friends thought it would ruin his career as a writer to banish himself to an obscure island in the Pacific Ocean. But he had little choice, for with his weakened lungs he was compelled to live in a mild climate. Time proved the wisdom of his decision, for in the tropical climate his health improved and, no doubt, years were added to his life. Instead of making him an exile, his withdrawal from the world caused the public to have an added interest in him and his writings.

Stevenson chose Samoa because it was less civilized than other places he had visited. Life in this primeval forest would have been uninteresting to most people, but to him it was fascinating. At first the Samoans were suspicious of the queer stranger who had come to live among them, but gradually he won them by kindness. After a time they came to regard him as a great chief to whom they could go with their problems.

The treaty of Berlin had made a great change in the lives of the Samoans. Instead of bringing them the advantages of civilization, it had brought oppression which was little better than slavery. Stevenson was always an idealist, and it was impossible for him to sit quietly by and see injustice meted out to the natives. He felt that fate had taken him to this island for a purpose, and that he had a mission to perform. He at once seized the opportunity to sacrifice himself for his fellow men and to have a part in a worthy cause. The fact that he was criticized for taking the part of the natives did not deter him from his purpose.

The natives soon found that Stevenson's advice was good and they came to him more and more often for counsel and advice. In spite of his efforts to keep down internal strife, a civil war broke out which resulted in the imprisonment of many of them. Stevenson's heart went out to them, for he realized what it meant to be shut up in prison for the rest of their lives. Even though it endangered his own health, he often visited them in their dungeons and carried them news of their families and the outside world.

When the war finally ended Stevenson begged for the release of these political prisoners. Those in authority said: "We have peace now for the first time in many months. These men are enemies of the government and are very dangerous. If we release them, war will break out again." But Stevenson replied: "You have peace because you yourself are different. These men have changed also, and they have promised me that, if they are released, they will not cause any more trouble."

When Stevenson finally brought about their release, they were so grateful that they wanted to repay the kindness in some way. Remembering that he had expressed a desire for a road from his home to a nearby highway, they decided not only to build this road, but to keep it in repair also. When some of the chiefs brought the news to him that the road was to be built as a token of appreciation from those he had befriended, Stevenson received the greatest surprise of his life.

Building a road through a jungle is not an easy task. The men were weak and pale from long confinement and unaccustomed to hard labor, but they were determined to build the road. In spite of their weakness they dug deep into the mire, and carried stones from a nearby mountain to make a firm roadbed. At times the heat of the sun was almost unbearable and their strength was nearly exhausted, but they worked unceasingly until the road was completed.

At the entrance of the road was placed this inscription:

THE ROAD OF GRATITUDE

CONSIDERING THE GREAT LOVE OF HIS EXCELLENCY, THE TELLER OF WONDROUS TALES, IN HIS LOVING CARE OF US IN OUR DISTRESS IN THE PRISON, WE HAVE PREPARED THIS SPLENDID GIFT. IT SHALL NEVER BE MUDDY, IT SHALL ENDURE FOREVER, THIS ROAD WHICH WE HAVE BUILT.

Stevenson did not live long to enjoy this splendid gift. Soon his friends were cutting another road over which he was to take his last earthly journey. The chiefs came and begged his body, which was carried on the shoulders of the strongest men to the summit of the mountain.

There, overlooking the sea, high above the haunts of men, is a stone marking his resting place, and engraved on it are these words which he wrote for his own epitaph:

Under the wide and starry sky,
Dig the grave and let me lie;
Glad did I live, and gladly die,
And I laid me down with a will.

This be the verse you grave for me:
Here he lies where he longed to be;
Home is the sailor, home from the sea,
And the hunter home from the hill.

In this country Stevenson is remembered as a great writer; but if you were to go to Samoa today, you would find his name engraved upon the hearts of the people because of his great kindness to them in their dire need. And the road which they built remains today as a token of their gratitude.

POEM: *"Wild Roars the Blast"* [32]

Wild roars the blast, the storm is high;
Above the storm are shining still
The lights by which we live and die;
Our peace is ever in Thy will.

What mighty hopes are in our care,
What holy dreams of brotherhood;
God of our fathers, help us dare
Their passion for the common good.

More light shall break from out thy word
For pilgrim followers of the gleam,
Till, led by Thy free spirit, Lord,
We see and share the pilgrim dream.

The ancient stars, the ancient faith,
Defend us till our voyage is done;
Across the floods of fear and death
The Mayflower still is sailing on.

—ALLEN EASTMAN CROSS.

PRAYER:

Heavenly Father, breathe into our hearts a love that will triumph over our prejudices. Forgive us that we have so long ignored the command of our Lord Jesus to love one another. Give us strength today to work a miracle in our hearts by intercession for those who seem to be enemies. Help all those who are living in fear to triumph in the love that casts out fear and creates a conquering faith. Grant to us this power that we may be like unto Jesus Christ, in whose name we pray. Amen.[33]

HYMN: *"O Zion, Haste."*

BENEDICTION.

GROUP IV

Great Stories Retold

SERVICE XII: THE GRASP OF THE FOOL

AIM: To lift up in the thinking of the group the comparison between material possessions and spiritual values.

INSTRUMENTAL PRELUDE: *"Evening Star"* from Tannhauser (WAGNER).

CALL TO WORSHIP (to be sung):

> From all that dwell below the skies,
> Let the Creator's praise arise;
> Let the Redeemer's name be sung,
> Through every land, by every tongue.
>
> In every land begin the song;
> To every land the strains belong:
> In cheerful sounds all voices raise,
> And fill the world with loudest praise.
> —ISAAC WATTS.

HYMN: *"God of Our Youth, to Whom We Yield,"* or
"Love Divine, All Loves Excelling,"
"Open My Eyes, That I May See."

RESPONSIVE READING:

Leader: And he said unto them, Take heed, and beware of covetousness: for a man's life consisteth not in the abundance of the things which he possesseth.

Response: And he spake a parable unto them, saying, The ground of a certain rich man brought forth plentifully:

Leader: And he thought within himself, saying, What shall I do, because I have no room where to bestow my fruits?

Response: And he said, This will I do: I will pull down my barns, and build greater; and there will I bestow all my fruits and my goods.

Leader: And I will say to my soul, Soul, thou hast much goods laid up for many years; take thine ease, eat, drink, and be merry.

Response: But God said unto him, Thou fool, this night thy soul shall be required of thee: then whose shall those things be, which thou hast provided? So is he that layeth up treasure for himself, and is not rich toward God.[34]

SPECIAL MUSIC: *"Lord, for Tomorrow and Its Needs."*
(Solo with violin and piano accompaniment.)

> Lord, for tomorrow and its needs
> I do not pray;
> Keep me, my God, from stain of sin
> Just for today.
>
> Help me to labor earnestly,
> And duly pray;
> Let me be kind in word and deed,
> Father, today.
>
> Let me no wrong nor idle word
> Unthinking say;
> Set Thou a seal upon my lips,
> Through all today.
>
> Lord, for tomorrow and its needs
> I do not pray;
> But keep me, guide me, love me, Lord,
> Through each today.
>
> —SYBIL F. PARTRIDGE.

STORY:

"HOW MUCH LAND DOES A MAN NEED?" [35]

PAHOM, the master of the house, sat listening to his wife as she talked with another woman. "It is perfectly true," thought he, "busy as we are from childhood, tilling the ground, we peasants never get ahead.

—92—

Our trouble is that we haven't enough land. If I had plenty of land, I shouldn't fear anything."

"Other people are buying," said he to his wife, "and we must also buy twenty acres or so." They had only one hundred rubles laid by, but they began to consider how they could manage to buy it. They decided to sell a colt, one-half of their bees, hire out one of their sons as a laborer and take his wages in advance, and borrow the rest of the purchase money.

Pahom then chose out a farm of forty acres and went to the lady to bargain for it. They came to an agreement, and he, paying a deposit in advance, agreed to pay the remainder within two years. Pahom now had land of his own.

The harvest was so good that within a year he had paid off his debts. When he went to plow his fields or to look at his growing corn, his heart filled with joy. The grass that grew and the flowers that bloomed there, seemed to him unlike any that grew elsewhere. Formerly, when he had passed by that land, it had appeared the same as any other, but now it seemed quite different.

About this time a rumor got about that many people were moving to new parts. One day a peasant, passing through the village, spent the night with Pahom. The stranger told him that some people, settling beyond the Volga, had joined the Commune and twenty-five acres had been granted to each man. The land was so good that the rye grew as high as a horse.

"Why should I suffer here, if one can live so well elsewhere? I will sell my land and with the money I will start afresh over there. But I must first go and find out all about it myself."

Toward the summer Pahom went down the Volga on a steamer to Samara, walked the rest of the way, and at last reached the place. It was just as the stranger had said. The peasants had plenty of land, and any one who had money could buy, at two shillings an acre, as much land as he wanted.

Having found out all he wished to know, Pahom returned home, sold off his belongings, and then started with his family for the new settlement. On his arrival five shares of land were given him for his own and his sons' use. He now had plenty of land.

At first, in the bustle of settling down, he was pleased with it all, but when he grew accustomed to it, he began to think that, even here, he had not enough land. One day a passing dealer, returned from the land of the Bashkirs, told him that in that far-away country he had bought thirteen thousand acres of land for one thousand rubles.

Pahom inquired how to get to the place; and, leaving immediately, he started on his journey, taking his man with him. When they reached the end of the journey the chief of the Bashkirs received him kindly, saying, "Choose whatever piece of land you like; we have plenty of it. Our price of land is always the same: one thousand rubles a day."

But Pahom did not understand. What measure is that? How many acres would that be?"

"We do not know how to reckon it out," said the chief. "We sell it by the day. As much as you can go round on your feet in a day is yours, and the price is one thousand rubles a day."

"But in a day you can get round a large tract of land," said Pahom.

"It will all be yours," replied the chief. "There is one condition, however. If you don't return on the same day to the spot where you started, your money is lost. We shall all go to any spot you like and stay there. You make your round, taking a spade with you. Wherever you think necessary, make a mark. At every turning dig a hole and pile up the turf; then afterwards we will go round with a plow from hole to hole. You may make as large a circuit as you please, but before the sun sets you must return to the place from which you started. All the land you cover will be yours."

Before daybreak Pahom was ready to start. As soon as they reached the plain the Chief stretched out his arm, saying, "As far as the eye can reach is our land. You may have any part of it." Taking off his cap, he continued: "This will be the mark. Start from here and return here again. All the land you go round shall be yours."

Pahom put his money in the cap, took off his outer coat, and, tying a flask of water to his girdle, started toward the rising sun. When it began to grow warm he took off another coat and his boots and stuck them in his girdle. "It will be easier walking now. I will go for another three miles," thought he, "and then turn to the left. This spot is so fine, it would be a pity to lose it. The farther one goes, the better the land seems."

When Pahom looked at the sun, he saw that it was nearly halfway to the horizon, and he was ten miles from his goal. "I must hurry back now in a straight line, and it will make my land lopsided. If only I had not tried for so much! What if I am too late?"

The next time he looked at the sun, it was near the rim. "What shall I do? I have grasped too much. I can't get there before the sun sets." Throwing away his coat, boots, and flask, he began running. His heart was beating like a hammer; and he was seized with terror lest he should die of the strain. Though afraid of death, he could not stop. At last he was near enough to hear the Bashkirs shouting to him.

Pahom rushed on; but just as he reached the hill, it suddenly grew dark. The sun had already set! He gave a cry: "All my labor has been in vain!" And he was about to stop when he heard the Bashkirs still shouting; and remembering that though to him the sun seemed to have set, they on the hill could still see it. Gathering his remaining strength, he at last reached the top, where he saw the Chief sitting beside the cap which held the money.

Pahom uttered a cry; his legs gave way beneath him, and as he fell forward his hands grasped the cap. "Ah, that's a fine fellow!" exclaimed the Chief. "He has gained much land."

Pahom's servant came running up and tried to raise him, but he saw that blood was flowing from his mouth. Pahom was dead!

The servant picked up the spade and dug a grave long enough for Pahom to lie in. Six feet from his head to his heels was all the land he needed.

PRAYER:

O God, Thou Source of all strength, we lift up our hearts to Thee in love and gratitude for the many things which Thou hast created for our pleasure. We come into Thy presence conscious of our unworthiness. We do not deserve the many gifts which have come from Thy hand. Forgive us if we have set our hearts upon temporal things, the things which cannot satisfy. Save us from greed, from covetousness, from unworthy desires. In the midst of distractions and confusions in the press of life grant that we may not lose a sense of Thy presence. Teach us how to be still and listen to Thy voice. Give unto us tranquillity, peace, and contentment. May we grow in spiritual vision and be enabled to discern eternal values. Give unto us the strength to take up our cross and follow Thee daily. In Jesus' name we pray. AMEN.

HYMN: *"Dear Lord and Father of Mankind."*

BENEDICTION (to be sung to the tune "Ellers").

> Saviour, again to Thy dear Name we raise
> With one accord our parting hymn of praise;
> We stand to bless Thee ere our worship cease;
> And still our hearts to wait Thy word of peace.
>
> Grant us Thy peace upon our homeward way;
> With Thee began, with Thee shall end the day:
> Guard Thou the lips from sin, the hearts from shame,
> That in this house have called upon Thy Name.
>
> —JOHN ELLERTON.

GROUP IV

Great Stories Retold

SERVICE XIII: THE PRICE OF A SOUL

AIM: To create an attitude of sympathy for those in need and a greater
desire to share the burdens of the weaker brother.

INSTRUMENTAL PRELUDE: *"Meditation"* from *"Thais"* (MASSENET).

CALL TO WORSHIP:

> Holy, holy, holy, Lord God of Hosts,
> Heaven and earth are full of Thy glory:
> Glory be to Thee, O Lord Most High.

HYMN: *"The Light of God Is Falling,"* or
"O Brother Man, Fold to Thy Heart."

SCRIPTURE READING:

Ye have heard that it hath been said, An eye for an eye, and a
tooth for a tooth: But I say unto you, That ye resist not evil: but
whosoever shall smite thee on thy right cheek, turn to him the other
also. And if any man will sue thee at the law, and take away thy
coat, let him have thy cloak also. And whosoever shall compel thee
to go a mile, go with him twain. Give to him that asketh thee, and
from him that would borrow of thee turn not thou away.

Therefore all things whatsoever ye would that men should do
to you, do ye even so to them: for this is the law and the prophets.[36]

STORY:

"THE BISHOP AND THE CANDLESTICKS" [37]

JEAN VALJEAN, a wood-chopper's son, was left an orphan when but a
child. His older sister reared him, but at the death of the sister's hus-

band Jean assumed the task of supporting the sister and her children. Although possessed of unusual strength for his seventeen years, he found it difficult to provide for all their needs, especially when his work was irregular.

One winter day, when he was without work, the children were crying for bread, and, when he could no longer withstand their entreaties, he went in search of food. Finally, in desperation, he broke a baker's window with his fist and carried home a loaf of bread to the hungry children. The next morning he was arrested for stealing—his bleeding hand was evidence sufficient to convict him.

For this crime he was sent to the galleys. Here an iron chain was riveted around his neck, to which was attached another chain that bound him to his galley seat. After four years he tried to escape, but was caught and three years were added to his sentence. A second attempt to escape added other years until he had served nineteen years.

When it came time to leave the galleys, Jean Valjean heard the strange words: "You are free." The moment seemed unreal. The ray of light which penetrated his soul soon faded; he had dreamed of a new life, but now he saw the sort of liberty that had come to him—a liberty with a yellow passport attached.

There were many bitter experiences in store for him. He had calculated that his savings during his stay at the galleys would amount to one hundred seventy-one francs. But this sum had been reduced by various local charges to one hundred nine francs and fifteen sous. When this was counted out to him on his departure, he felt that the state had robbed him, not only of the best years of his life, but of his meager savings as well. These with other wrongs embittered him, until his heart was hardened and he was more like an animal than a man.

When Jean Valjean was released it seemed that every man's hand was against him. Wherever he went he was considered a dangerous man and was promptly driven away. At the inn the keeper would not receive him because he knew him to be a convict. He would neither allow Jean to sleep in the kennel nor give him the food intended for the dogs.

Finally he came to the home of a good bishop who gave him a bed for the night. Not being accustomed to a bed, he lay awake for hours. Since he could not sleep he began to think. Among other thoughts this one continually presented itself: He had noticed the six silver plates that had been put on the table the evening before.

The idea of owning those plates took possession of him. He had watched the old servant as she placed them in a little cupboard. They were solid and, with the ladle, would bring at least two hundred francs—and that was twice what he had received for nineteen years of hard labor.

All was still in the house. He went to the window and found that it had no bars, but that it opened upon a garden which was surrounded by a low wall. He took his drill out of his knapsack, put his shoes in his pocket, and moved toward the bishop's room. He found it unlatched, so he pushed the door open. A deep calm filled the room. As he moved cautiously, avoiding the pieces of furniture, he could hear the quiet breathing of the sleeping bishop. As he glanced at him his pale face was lighted up by a ray of moonlight from a high window. There was something of divinity about him; his white locks gave him a serene and majestic glory.

As Jean Valjean stood over the bishop, there was a strange indecision. He was ready either to cleave his skull or to kiss his hand as it hung over the side of the bed. Instead, he walked quickly over to the cupboard, took the silver, ran across the garden, leaped over the wall, and fled.

The next morning the woman who served the bishop informed him that the silver had been stolen by the man who had lodged there the previous night. The bishop answered very mildly: "I have for a long time wrongfully withheld this silver, for it really belongs to the poor. And who was this man? Evidently a poor man!"

As they were breakfasting without silver, the bishop pleasantly remarked that there was really no need even of a wooden spoon or fork to dip a piece of bread into a cup of milk.

"Was there ever such an idea?" the servant remarked, "to take in a man like that, to give him a bed and food? Yet it is a blessing that he did nothing but steal!"

Just then the door opened and a strange group appeared. One of the officers was holding Jean Valjean by the collar.

The bishop hurried to the door and, speaking to Valjean, said: "Ah, there you are! But I gave you the candlesticks also, which are silver like the rest, and would bring at least two hundred francs. Why did you not take them along with your plates?"

Valjean looked at the bishop with an expression which no human tongue could describe.

"Sir," said the officer, "then what this man said was true?"

"Yes, just as he told you—that the silver had been given him by an old priest with whom he had spent the night. Why did you bring him back? It is all a mistake!"

"If that is so," said the officer, "then we can let him go."

"Yes," replied the bishop.

"Is it true that they will let me go?" said Jean Valjean.

"Yes, you can go," said the officer.

"My friend," said the bishop, "before you go away, here are your candlesticks; take them." He went to the mantelpiece and brought them to Jean Valjean who took them mechanically as if in a daze. He was trembling in every limb.

"Now," said the bishop, "go in peace. By the way, when you come again you need not come through the garden. You can always come in by the front door; it is closed only with a latch, day or night."

Jean Valjean felt like a man who is just about to faint. The bishop approached him and said in a low voice: "Jean Valjean, my brother, you belong no longer to evil, but to good. It is your soul I am buying with these candlesticks. Do not forget that you have promised me to use this silver to become an honest man." But he had no recollection of that promise.

Years later, however, when Jean Valjean was a respectable citizen and the leading man of his community, he realized that Christ had come to him through the influence of the good bishop.

HYMN: *"Lift Up Our Hearts"*

Lift up our hearts, O King of kings,
To brighter hopes and kindlier things,
To visions of a larger good,
And holier dreams of brotherhood.

The world is weary of its pain,
Of selfish greed and fruitless gain,
Of tarnished honor, falsely strong,
Of all its ancient deeds of wrong.

Almighty Father, who dost give
The gift of life to all who live,
Look down on all earth's sin and strife,
And lift us to a nobler life.
—JOHN H. B. MASTERMAN.

PRAYER:

O Thou who art the Father of us all, reveal unto us the things we can do to free the world from oppression and to bring justice to all people, regardless of race, color, or creed. Grant that we may have a real concern for those we have previously ignored or neglected. Forgive us for our indifference toward the suffering of others, and for our selfishness which blinds us to the needs of those about us. Grant that we may do all in our power to hasten the day when the exploited and the weak, the backward and the downtrodden, will have an equal chance with those who are more favored. In the name of Jesus, we pray. AMEN.

BENEDICTION.

GROUP IV

Great Stories Retold

SERVICE XIV: INASMUCH

AIM: To lead to a conscious sharing of God's purpose for us through ministering to the needs of others.

PRELUDE: Music to Hymn tune, *"Germany."*

CALL TO WORSHIP:

Leader: The Lord is gracious, and full of compassion; slow to anger, and of great loving-kindness. The Lord is good to all; and his tender mercies are over all his works.

Response: O come, let us worship and bow down;
Let us kneel before the Lord our Maker.

HYMN: *"God of the Strong"*

God of the strong, God of the weak,
Lord of all lands and our own land,
Light of all souls: from Thee we seek
Light from Thy light, strength from Thy hand.

In suffering Thou hast made us one,
In mighty burdens one are we:
Teach us that lowliest duty done
Is highest service unto Thee.

Teach us, great Teacher of mankind,
The sacrifice that brings Thy balm:
The love, the work that bless and bind;
Teach us Thy majesty, Thy calm.
                           —RICHARD WATSON GILDER.

SCRIPTURE READING:

Then shall the King say unto them on his right hand, Come, ye blessed of my Father, inherit the kingdom prepared for you from the foundation of the world: for I was an hungred, and ye gave me meat: I was thirsty, and ye gave me drink: I was a stranger, and ye took me in: naked, and ye clothed me: I was sick, and ye visited me: I was in prison, and ye came unto me. Then shall the righteous answer him, saying, Lord, when saw we thee an hungred, and fed thee? or thirsty, and gave thee drink? when saw we thee a stranger, and took thee in? or naked, and clothed thee? or when saw we thee sick, or in prison, and came unto thee? And the King shall answer and say unto them, Verily I say unto you, Inasmuch as ye have done it unto one of the least of these my brethren, ye have done it unto me.[38]

PRAYER:

Our Father, who carest for all Thy children alike, help us to look upon every person, regardless of class or color, as our brother. Forgive us that we have so long ignored Thy command to love one another. Give unto us that perfect love which will enable us to triumph over all differences, all hatred and prejudice. As we hear Thy call to share with those about us, may we not close our ears to the calls of the discouraged or to the cries of the distressed. Awaken within us a desire to extend a helping hand to those who are in need as we strive to serve Thee through ministering unto our fellow man. In the name of Jesus, the Master of all men, we pray. AMEN.

STORY:

"UNTO ONE OF THE LEAST" [39]

ABOUT NOON, on a calm summer's day, a party of ten horsemen drew near the village of Nazareth. They came from the south, evidently from Jerusalem. A trumpet, sounded when the cavalcade drew near the village, had a magical effect upon the inhabitants. They crowded to their doors and gates eager to be the first to catch the meaning of the unusual visit, for Nazareth was away from the main highroad, and travelers were seldom seen.

The approaching horsemen were soon discovered to be Roman soldiers, led by a decurion, or captain of ten. Much as the villagers hated the Romans, curiosity brought them into the streets, and they followed the procession to the well at the northeastern corner of the little straggling village, where they knew the soldiers would dismount.

As they followed, they observed a prisoner bound by his wrists to the saddle of one of the horsemen. He was afoot, stooped with exhaustion, and almost suffocated by the yellow dust, which rose in clouds as the horses proceeded. As they halted he sank to the ground in a stupor, unheeded by his captors.

The villagers were interested in him at once, especially as they saw that he was young, a mere boy. They would have helped him had they dared, but fear of the Roman soldiers held them back.

As the soldiers were drinking at the well, a woman cried out, "Look! Yonder comes the carpenter. Now we will hear something." Evidently the person referred to was of some importance in the village. He was quite venerable in appearance. Thin white locks fell below the edge of his turban, and a mass of still whiter beard flowed down the front of his coarse gray gown. He carried crude carpenter tools, and was followed by a young apprentice carrying an ax. As he drew near he stopped to survey the group.

"O Rabbi Joseph," cried one of the villagers, "come and ask the soldiers about this prisoner. See, he has fallen, and no one cares for him."

The rabbi glanced at the prisoner, and presently approached the decurion.

"Peace be unto you," he said gravely.

"And unto you," the decurion replied.

"And you come from Jerusalem?"

"Yes."

"Your prisoner is young. May I ask what he has done?"

"The charge against him is that he attempted the life of a Roman officer. He claims it was an accident, but the charge was laid against him nevertheless."

"Is he a Jew?"

"His father was a prince of Jerusalem in Herod's time, named Hur—Ben-Hur, I believe they called him. In the streets of Jerusalem, day before yesterday, he nearly killed the noble Gratus by flinging a tile upon his head from the roof of a palace—his father's, I believe.

There was a pause in the conversation during which the Nazarenes gazed at the young Ben-Hur as at a wild beast.

"Is he under sentence?"

"Yes, the galleys for life."

"The Lord have mercy on him!" exclaimed the rabbi earnestly.

At these words the young apprentice who accompanied Joseph laid down the ax and, going to the well, took from it a pitcher of water. The action was so quiet that, before the guards could interfere, he was stooping over the prisoner, offering him a drink.

At the kindly touch upon his shoulder the prisoner awoke and, looking upward, saw a face that he never forgot—the face of a boy about his own age. He looked into deep blue eyes, full of love and sympathy, yet with a certain dignity and power. He drank deeply of the cool water. The young lad did not speak to him, but it seemed as though the spirit of the prisoner, hardened by cruelty, injustice, and thoughts of revenge, softened under that kindly glance.

When the draught was finished, the hand that had been resting upon the prisoner's shoulder was lifted to his head, and remained upon the dusty locks long enough to say a blessing. The stranger then returned the pitcher to its place at the well, and, taking his ax again, went back to Rabbi Joseph. All eyes went with him, the decurion's as well as those of the villagers.

As the soldiers remounted they, too, seemed in a better temper, for the decurion loosened the bonds of the prisoner and set him on a horse behind one of the soldiers. The Nazarenes went to their homes, and Joseph and the lad to their work.

In giving the drink of water, Jesus of Nazareth had ministered unto one of the least of his brethren.

A SOCIAL LITANY:

Leader: From all hatred, all class bitterness, all prejudice, or any other sins which would separate us from Thee,

Response: O God, deliver us.

Leader: From all legalized cruelty, from greed, and from all inconsiderate ways which would grind out the lives of men,

Response: O God, deliver us.

Leader: From the selfishness which makes some men rich at the expense of others,

Response: O God, deliver us.

Leader: Strengthen our sense of justice and our regard for the worth of human life,

Response: O God, we pray.

Leader: Grant that our spirit may cry out against injustice wherever
  it is tolerated,
Response: O God, we pray.
Leader: Help us as we strive to live as brothers to all people,
Response: In Jesus' name, we pray. AMEN.

POEM: *"O Jesus, Master, When Today"* [40]

> O Jesus, Master, when today
>   I meet along the crowded way
> My burdened brothers—mine and Thine—
>   May then through me Thy Spirit shine;
>
> To cheer them in their onward way,
>   Till evening ends the varied day;
> To kindle so a growing light
>   Where else might be but gloom and night.
>
> Grant, too, that they my need may know,
>   As side by side we onward go:
> An equal need of kindly thought
>   And love like that which Thou hast taught.
>
> —CHARLES S. NEWHALL.

BENEDICTION:

The grace of our Lord Jesus Christ, the love of God, and the
fellowship of the Holy Spirit be with us all evermore.

Great Stories Retold

SERVICE XV: ACHIEVEMENT OF GREATNESS

AIM: To lead to a clearer understanding of the meaning of true greatness, and to a desire to choose the best which life has to offer.

INSTRUMENTAL PRELUDE: *"With Verdure Clad,"* from *"Creation"*
(HADYN).

CALL TO WORSHIP:

Leader: Know ye not that ye are the temple of God, and that the
Spirit of God dwelleth in you? For as many as are led by the
Spirit of God, they are the children of God. God is a Spirit: and
they that worship him must worship him in spirit and in truth.

Response: O come, let us worship and bow down, let us kneel before
the Lord our maker.

HYMN: *"Teach Me, My God and King,"* or
"Awake, My Soul, Stretch Every Nerve,"
"Christ of the Upward Way."

SCRIPTURE READING (in unison):

Blessed is the man that walketh not in the counsel of the
wicked,
Nor standeth in the way of sinners,
Nor sitteth in the seat of the scornful.
But his delight is in the law of the Lord;
And in his law doth he meditate day and night.

And he shall be like a tree planted by the streams of water,
That bringeth its fruit in its season;
Whose leaf also doth not wither;
And whatsoever he doeth shall prosper.
The wicked are not so,
But are like the chaff which the wind driveth away.

Therefore the wicked shall not stand in the judgment,
Nor sinners in the congregation of the righteous.
For the Lord knoweth the way of the righteous;
But the way of the wicked shall perish.[41]

STORY:

"THE GREAT STONE FACE" [42]

ONE AFTERNOON a mother and her son sat at the door of their cottage talking about the Great Stone Face. They had but to lift their eyes and there it was plainly to be seen, though miles away, with the sunshine brightening all its features.

The Great Stone Face was a work of Nature in her mood of majestic playfulness, formed on the perpendicular side of a mountain by some immense rocks, which viewed at a distance resembled the human countenance. It seemed as if an enormous giant had sculptured his own likeness on the precipice. There was the broad arch of the forehead, the nose with its long bridge, and the vast lips, which, if they could have spoken, would have rolled their thunder accents from one end of the valley to the other.

It was a happy lot for children to grow up with the Great Stone Face before their eyes, for all the features were noble, and the expression was at once grand and sweet, as if it were the glow of a vast, warm heart that embraced all mankind in its affection. It was an education only to look at it.

As the mother and son sat gazing at the Great Stone Face, Ernest said: "Mother, I wish it could speak, for it looks so very kindly that its voice must be pleasant."

"If an old prophecy should come to pass," answered the mother, "we may see a man, sometime or other, with exactly such a face as that."

"What prophecy do you mean, mother?" eagerly inquired Ernest. So his mother told him a story that her own mother had told to her, a story so old that even the Indians had heard it from their fore-fathers. As the story goes, at some future day a child should be born who was destined to become the greatest and noblest personage of his time, and whose features in manhood should resemble the Great Stone Face. Many still believed in the prophecy, but the great man had not yet appeared.

"Mother, I do hope I shall live to see him," said Ernest.

"Perhaps you may," answered his mother.

Ernest never forgot the story. It was always in his mind when he looked upon the Great Stone Face. When the toil of the day was over he would gaze at it for hours, until he began to imagine that those vast features recognized him and gave him a smile of kindness and encouragement. The secret was that the boy saw what others could not see, and thus the love which was meant for all became his peculiar portion.

About this time a rumor spread throughout the valley that the great man had come at last. Many years ago a young man had migrated from the valley and settled at a distant seaport. Being shrewd and active, he had become exceedingly rich, and remembering his native valley, he had decided to return and end his days where he had been born.

Ernest was deeply stirred by the story, but when he saw the man he turned away and gazed at those glorious features which had impressed themselves in his soul. The benign lips seemed to say: "He will come! Fear not, the man will come!"

It happened that a native-born son of the valley many years before had enlisted as a soldier and had now returned an illustrious commander. At a great public dinner the speakers acclaimed him the greatest man of this or any other age. But Ernest could not see the resemblance to the Great Stone Face. "This is not the man of prophecy," sighed Ernest; "the world must wait longer yet. Surely he will appear as a man of peace, uttering words of wisdom, doing good and making people happy."

As the years passed Ernest gradually became known among the people. He still labored for his daily bread and was the same simple-hearted man that he had always been. But he had thought and felt so much that he had gained wisdom unawares. Not a day passed that the world was not made better because he lived. He never stepped aside from his path, yet he would always reach a blessing to his neighbor. The simplicity of his thought took shape in his good deeds and showed in his speech. He uttered truths that molded the lives of those who heard him. No one suspected that he was more than an ordinary man; least of all did Ernest himself suspect it.

Ernest was now an aged man, but he had not grown old in vain. Fame had come to him, for he was known beyond the limits of the valley. Great men came from afar to talk to him because his ideas were unlike those of other men.

The songs of a new poet found their way to Ernest. As he read them, he lifted his eyes to the Great Stone Face and said: "Majestic friend, is not this man worthy to resemble thee?" The face seemed to smile, but answered not a word.

It happened that the poet had heard of Ernest and had thought much of his untaught wisdom and noble simplicity of life. The poet sought out Ernest and found him sitting by the cottage door reading a volume of his poems. As they talked together, Ernest examined the poet's features; then turned to the Great Stone Face; then back, with uncertainty, to his guest. But his countenance fell; he shook his head and sighed.

"Wherefore are you sad?" inquired the poet.

"Because," replied Ernest, "all through life I have waited for the fulfilment of a prophecy, and when I read these poems, I hoped it might be fulfilled in you."

"You hoped," answered the poet, "to find in me the likeness of the Great Stone Face, and you are disappointed. Yes, it is my doom. For in shame and sadness do I speak it: I am not worthy to resemble that majestic image."

"And why?" asked Ernest as he pointed to the poems; "are not those thoughts divine?"

"But my life does not correspond with my thoughts. I have had great dreams; but they have been only dreams, because I have lived, by my own choice, among poor and mean realities. Sometimes even I lack faith in the grandeur, beauty, and goodness which my works are said to contain. Why, then, should you hope to find in me yonder image of the divine?" The poet spoke sadly.

At the hour of sunset, as had long been his custom, Ernest was to speak to the people of the neighborhood in the open air. He and the poet, still talking together, came to the spot. It was a small nook among the hills. At a slight elevation above the ground, there was a

— 110 —

niche large enough to admit a figure. From this natural pulpit **Ernest** spoke to the people as they sat upon the grass. In another direction the Great Stone Face could be seen.

As Ernest began to speak his words had power because **his** thoughts harmonized with his life. The poet, as he listened, felt that Ernest represented a nobler strain of poetry than anything he had **ever** written. At that moment, in sympathy with a thought which he **was** about to utter, the face of Ernest assumed a grandeur of expression. The poet, by an irresistible impulse, threw his arms aloft and shouted: "Behold! Ernest is himself the likeness of the Great Stone Face."

Then all the people looked and saw what the poet said was true. The prophecy was fulfilled. But Ernest, having finished what he had to say, took the poet's arm and walked slowly homeward, still hoping that some wiser and better man than himself would appear, bearing a resemblance to the GREAT STONE FACE.

PRAYER:

O Lord of Love, kindle in our souls Thy fire of love. Help us to love Thee with all our heart, soul, strength and mind and our neighbor as ourselves. Help us to be meek and lowly in heart. Sweeten our temper and dispose us to be kind and helpful to all. Make us kind in thought, gentle in speech, and generous in action. Teach us that it is more blessed to give than to receive; that it is better to minister than to be ministered unto; better to forget ourselves than to put ourselves forward. Deliver us from anger and from envy; from all harsh thoughts and unlovely manners. Make us of some use in this world; may we more and more forget ourselves in glad service for Thee. AMEN.[43]

HYMN: *"Love Thyself Last,"* or
"Great Master, Touch Us,"
"Be Thou My Vision."

BENEDICTION:

Hasten the time, O Lord, when all the earth shall be full of Thy glory. AMEN.

Great Stories Retold

SERVICE XVI: PROCRASTINATION

AIM: To lead to a desire to use one's time and talents to the best advantage, applying one's self to the tasks near at hand.

INSTRUMENTAL PRELUDE: *"Ave Maria"* (BACH-GOUNOD, piano and violin).

CALL TO WORSHIP:

"Holy, Holy, Holy," from "The Holy City," by Alfred R. Gaul. (Tune, "Sanctus.")

Holy, holy, holy, Lord of hosts:
Holy, holy, holy is the Lord of hosts. Amen.

RESPONSIVE READING:

Leader: God be merciful unto us, and bless us; and cause his face to shine upon us.

Response: That thy way may be known upon earth, thy saving health among all nations.

Leader: Let the people praise thee, O God; let all the people praise thee.

Response: O let the nations be glad and sing for joy.

Leader: For thou shalt judge the people righteously, and govern the nations upon earth.

Response: Let the people praise thee, O God; let all the people praise thee.

Leader: Then shall the earth yield her increase; and God, even our own God, shall bless us.

Response: God shall bless us; and all the ends of the earth shall fear him.[44]

HYMN: *"Heralds of Christ."*

SCRIPTURE:

And it shall come to pass afterward, that I will pour out my spirit upon all flesh; and your sons and your daughters shall prophesy, your old men shall dream dreams, your young men shall see visions.

Where there is no vision, the people perish.

I saw the Lord, sitting upon the throne, high and lifted up, and his train filled the temple. Above him stood the seraphim; and one cried unto another, and said, Holy, holy, holy, is the Lord of hosts: the whole earth is full of his glory.

Then flew one of the seraphim unto me, having a live coal in his hand; and he touched my mouth with it.

And I heard the voice of the Lord, saying, Whom shall I send, and who will go for us? Then said I, Here am I; send me.[45]

POEM: *"Thank God for Fools"* [46]

Thank God for fools!—for men who dare to dream
  Beyond the lean horizon of their days;
Men not too timid to pursue the gleam
  To unguessed lands of wonder and amaze.

Thank God for fools! The trails that ring the world
  Are dark with blood and sweat where they have passed.
There are the flags of every crag unfurled;
  Theirs—ashes and oblivion at last.

Thank God for fools!—abused, of low estate.
  We rear our temples on the stones they laid;
Ours is the prize their tired souls might not wait;
  Theirs—the requiem of the unafraid.

                                       —ANONYMOUS.

STORY:

"THE MADONNA OF THE FUTURE" [47]

I HAD ARRIVED late in Florence, and was wandering in the heart of the city when I came upon Michelangelo's statue of "David." I turned from his sinister strength to a slender person standing near who asked me for my impression. I knew at once that he was an artist. He seemed picturesque, but slightly unreal. I learned that he was a New Yorker—one who was probably waiting for an inspiration.

When I inquired, he said: "Yes, I'm at work night and day. I've undertaken a creation, but my studio has never been profaned by superficial, feverish, mercenary work. It is a temple of labor, but also of leisure. Art is long; if we work for ourselves, we must hurry; but if we work for her, we must often pause. She can wait. Visions are rare; we must look long to see them."

As we walked through the art galleries, pausing before the masterpieces of past ages, he seemed enthusiastic. Stopping before one of them, he said: "My picture may be great! Think of being known to mankind after some such fashion as this! Of hanging here through the slow centuries in the gaze of the world! I don't often mention my picture, but there's nothing grotesque in a pure ambition, or in a life devoted to it."

I was impressed with my companion's singleness of purpose. He seemed to move in his own little province of art. Just as a truly religious soul is always at worship, the genuine artist is always at labor. He seemed never to be idle, but always gathering treasures to pour into the lap of his Madonna.

Later I was introduced to an American lady whose home was a place of reunion for foreign residents. I asked her if she knew my friend, Mr. Theobold, the artist. She replied: "Know him! All Florence knows him, and his wondrous Madonna!"

"Really, you don't believe in his Madonna?"

"We all believed in him once. All the women were anxious to sit for him, but the months passed by, and he never produced his masterpiece. He would say, 'Great work requires time and contemplation.' But none of us have ever seen his painting."

I thought probably the American lady had exaggerated, but one day Theobold presented me to his model. She was indeed a beautiful woman, I saw, after recovering from the surprise of finding her without the freshness of youth. Once there might have been a dim spiritual light in her face, but it had long since begun to fade.

Then he told me how he discovered her: "I was coming in one summer night from a walk in the country when I met this mother with her baby. She looked as if she had stepped out of the stable in Bethlehem. She was the most beautiful creature I had ever looked upon; the most saintly expression upon her face. Since then I have studied her; I've absorbed her little by little. Now I have determined to clinch the impression. I shall at last invite her to sit for me!"

"At last! at last! Do you mean that she has never done so yet?" I asked in astonishment.

"I've not really had a sitting. I've taken notes; I've gotten my grand fundamental impression. That's the great thing! But I've not actually had her before my easel as a model."

"My poor friend," I exclaimed, "you have dawdled! She's an old, old woman for a Madonna!"

He drew a long breath, grasping my arm. "Answer me solemnly: Does she seem old? Is she wrinkled? Is she faded? Am I blind?"

Then at last I understood the immensity of his illusion—how one by one the noiseless years had ebbed away, and left him brooding in charmed inaction, forever dreaming about his work and preparing for it, but always deferring it. It seemed a kindness not to tell him the plain truth.

"I should be sorry to say you are blind, but I think you've lost time in effortless contemplation. Your Madonna was once young and fresh, but that was some years ago."

"Old, old!" he kept repeating. "Has life been a dream? Have I worshiped too long? Have I loved too well?"

The charm was broken! That the cord of illusion should have snapped at my light touch showed how it had been weakened by excessive tension. The poor fellow's sense of wasted time, of vanished opportunities seemed to roll in upon his soul in waves of darkness. He suddenly dropped his head and burst into tears.

I led him home with all possible tenderness. Before a week had passed we buried him in the little Protestant cemetery on the way to Fiesole. The *Madonna of the Future* was never painted.

POEM: *"Great Master, Touch Us"*

> Great Master, touch us with Thy skilful hands;
>   Let not the music that is in us die:
> Great Sculptor, hew and polish us, nor let,
>   Hidden and lost, Thy form within us lie.
>
> Spare not the stroke; do with us what Thou wilt;
>   Let there be naught unfinished, broken, marred;

Complete Thy purpose that we may become
Thy perfect image—Thou our God and Lord.
—Horatius Bonar.

LITANY OF CONFESSION:

Leader: For the visions which have come to thy servants of old,
Response: We thank thee, our Father.
Leader: That these great leaders labored faithfully and passed on to us
the unfinished tasks,
Response: We thank thee, our Father.
Leader: As we receive this commission of Thy hands, help us to determine to labor diligently that we may fulfill Thy purpose.
Response: Hear our prayer, our Father.
Leader: We have heard Thy voice calling us to special tasks, but we
have not always been prompt in our obedience.
Response: Forgive us, our Father.
Leader: We have often done the things which we ought not to have
done, and have left undone the things which we ought to have
done.
Response: Forgive us, O God, for our failures.
Leader: Grant unto us a new insight into Thy truth and a vision of
the tasks near at hand.
Response: Hear our prayer, O God.
Leader: Open our eyes that we may not be blinded by doubt, or confused by conflicting desires.
Response: Hear our prayer, O God.
Leader: Grant that with motives pure and with a purpose true we may
labor courageously that honor may come to Thy name,
Response: We humbly pray, O God.
Leader: Fill us with Thy spirit that we may resolve steadfastly to follow Thee,
Response: In the name of the Master of all men, we pray. Amen.

HYMN: *"Pass On the Torch,"* or

"To the Knights in the Days of Old."

BENEDICTION:

Now may the light that shone in Jesus Christ, our Lord,
Shine in our hearts and minds by the indwelling Word;
And may the radiance which faith and hope restore,
Be and abide with us both now and forever more. Amen.

SERVICE XVII: TO WHAT PURPOSE?

AIM: To lead to a desire to find God's purpose for one's life and to follow it resolutely.

INSTRUMENTAL PRELUDE: *"Melody in F"* (RUBINSTEIN).

CALL TO WORSHIP:

> Let all the world in every corner sing,
>   "My God and King!"
> The heavens are not too high,
> His praise may thither fly;
> The earth is not too low,
> His praises there may grow,
> Let all the world in every corner sing,
>   "My God and King!"
>   —GEORGE HERBERT.

HYMN: *"Praise the Lord! Ye Heavens, Adore Him."*

SCRIPTURE READING:

And when he was gone forth into the way, there came one running, and kneeled to him, and asked him, Good Master, what shall I do that I may inherit eternal life? And Jesus said unto him, Why callest thou me good? there is none good but one, that is, God. Thou knowest the commandments, Do not commit adultery, Do not kill, Do not steal, Do not bear false witness, Defraud not, Honor thy father and mother. And he answered and said unto him, Master, all these have I observed from my youth. Then Jesus beholding him loved him, and said unto him, One thing thou lackest: go thy way, sell whatsoever thou hast, and give to the poor, and thou shalt have treasure in heaven: and come, take up the cross, and follow me. And he was sad at that saying, and went away grieved: for he had great possessions.[48]

STORY:

"CHRIST AND THE RICH YOUNG RULER"
(PICTURE INTERPRETATION)[49]

FEW NAMES in the world of modern art are more favorably known than that of Hofmann (1824-1902), the German artist. His paintings cover a wide field, but his success was greatest with religious subjects. His scenes from the life of Christ are widely known, due to the fact that they are constantly used as illustrations for Church school literature. It has been said that his pictures of Christ are the most beautiful in the history of art.

In his picture, "Christ and the Rich Young Ruler," Hofmann has given us the only notable portrayal of this incident in the life of Christ. It was painted as a result of inspiration which came from reading the account in the Scriptures.

In this picture the artist has portrayed the fine features of the Master, his open countenance and commanding presence which express his divine intelligence. In the face of the young ruler there is a longing yet inquiring look, a face filled with an earnest desire. But as one studies the picture his attention is drawn again to the supreme attraction in the picture, the Master, who with a kingly presence and a calm dignity is certainly impressing the rich young ruler.

Hofmann has immortalized the most dramatic incident in the life of Christ in this picture. The young man is inquiring of Jesus the way of life; Jesus is pleased at his desire to find life. His face shows refinement, yet it is not strong. He is dressed as a ruler should be; his clothes are in excellent taste.

In the background we see a crippled beggar asking for alms and a woman also seeking help. What relation do they bear to the young ruler? Perhaps the artist is trying to show us two ways of living: the luxury and wealth of the young man and the wretchedness and poverty of the beggars.

The young ruler came to Jesus with a great longing in his heart, feeling sure that here was one who could answer the question that had been puzzling him. He came running and knelt before Jesus.

His eagerness must have appealed to the Master, who immediately loved him and wanted him for his disciple. Here were the very qualities which Jesus needed in building his Kingdom.

The young man had wealth and power; yet, in spite of these things, he was not happy. There was something lacking—a vague hunger for which he had not been able to find satisfaction. Surely Jesus could help him, so he inquires, "What must I do to be sure of eternal life?"

Jesus, pointing to the needs of the world, the poor, the crippled, says to the young man, "Go, sell all your goods; give to the poor; and come, follow me." The young man had not thought of his possessions as a means of serving Jesus. He was honest in believing that he had kept all the commandments, yet he had been indifferent to the needs of the poor. He had set his heart upon material things, because he valued most the things which money could buy.

Notice how the eyes of Jesus are searching the soul of the young man. He is looking at him with eyes of kindness and of love. He sees the issues that are involved—the difference that it will make in the life of the young man if his goods are divided with those who are in need. Jesus sees him as a young man who has mastered himself, but has not found a cause in which to lose himself.

The young man is not willing to meet the issue. The eagerness has gone from his face; dejection and disillusionment are clearly written in his whole manner. He sees the challenge, but will not accept it. Instead he bows his head, saying to himself: "Some other time—not now." Then he turns and walks away. By deferring the problem, he lost the opportunity of being probably the most prominent of the disciples. Today he is known to us simply as an anonymous young man.

POEM:

> Once to every man and nation comes the moment to decide,
> In the strife of truth with falsehood, for the good or evil side;
> Some great cause, God's new Messiah, offering each the bloom or
>   blight,
> Parts the goats upon the left hand and the sheep upon the right,
> And the choice goes by forever 'twixt that darkness and that
>   light.[50]

—JAMES RUSSELL LOWELL.

DIRECTED MEDITATION:

In the quietness of this hour, let us search our hearts and lives to see what it is that keeps us from becoming a consecrated follower of Jesus. While it was great possessions in the case of this young man, it may be indifference, lack of purpose, or it may be that we lack courage to follow Truth unafraid. . . . (pause) . . . . Or it may be the influence of the crowd, or the fear of what others may say if we dare to follow our best impulses . . . . (pause) . . . . Are we willing to forego the pleasure of the moment for a more lasting satisfaction later on? . . . (pause) . . . If necessary, are we willing to go back and retrace our steps until we come to the place where we turned aside to follow the line of least resistance? . . . (Pause). Let us be absolutely honest and put away all pretense, as we ask God to reveal to us anything in our lives which would keep us from wholehearted devotion to His cause.

LITANY OF YOUTH:

Leader: O God, who through Thy Son, Jesus of Nazareth, hast changed the civilization of the world, we have heard Thy voice calling us to forsake all and follow Thee.

Response: O God, may we heed this call.

Leader: O Thou, who hast called to the youth of every age, may we put out of our lives all low desires and all sins of omission or commission which would keep us from following Thee.

Response: O God, deliver us from low choices.

Leader: From unbelief, purposeless living, low tastes, and sensual desires,

Response: Deliver us, O God.

Leader: Grant that we may guard our character and preserve our integrity against all evil influences. May we go forth with all the zest and radiance of youth to live as Jesus taught us. Give us courage to accept this challenge.

Response: In Jesus' name, we pray. AMEN.

HYMN: *"O Young and Fearless Prophet"* [51]

O young and fearless Prophet of ancient Galilee:
Thy life is still a summons to serve humanity,
To make our thoughts and actions less prone to please the crowd,
To stand with humble courage for Truth with hearts uncowed.

We marvel at the purpose that held Thee to Thy course
While ever on the hilltop before Thee loomed the cross;
Thy steadfast face set forward where love and duty shone,
While we betray so quickly and leave Thee there alone.

Create in us the splendor that dawns when hearts are kind,
That knows not race nor station as boundaries of the mind;
That learns to value beauty, in heart, or brain, or soul,
And longs to bind God's children into one perfect whole.

O young and fearless Prophet, we need Thy presence here,
Amid our pride and glory to see Thy face appear;
Once more to hear Thy challenge above our noisy day,
Again to lead us forward along God's holy way.

—S. RALPH HARLOW.

BENEDICTION:

Let the words of my mouth, and the meditation of my heart, be
acceptable in thy sight, O Lord, my strength, and my redeemer.

SERVICE XVIII: HANDS THAT SERVE

AIM: To lead to a greater desire to give oneself in service to others.

INSTRUMENTAL PRELUDE: *"Serenade"* (SCHUBERT).

CALL TO WORSHIP:

Leader: Lift up your hearts.

Response: We lift them up unto the Lord.

Leader: O Lord, open thou our eyes,

Response: That we may behold wondrous things out of thy law.

Leader: O Lord, open thou our lips,

Response: And our mouth shall show forth thy praise.

Leader: Praise ye the Lord.

Response: The Lord's name be praised. From the rising sun to the going down of the same, the Lord's name is to be praised.

Leader: Let our prayers be set forth as incense before him, the lifting up of our hands as the evening sacrifice.

Response: Let the people praise thee, O God; let all the people praise thee.

HYMN: *"O Master, Let Me Walk with Thee,"* or
"We Thank Thee, Lord, Thy Paths of Service,"
"Go, Labor On, Spend and Be Spent."

RESPONSIVE READING:

Leader: This is the message that ye heard from the beginning, that we should love one another.

Response: No man liveth unto himself.

Leader: He that loveth not his brother whom he hath seen, how can he love God whom he hath not seen?

Response: We know that we have passed from death unto life, because we love the brethren.

Leader: Let us not love in word, neither in tongue but in deed and truth.

Response: This is my commandment, That ye love one another, as I have loved you.

Leader: There is no fear in love, but perfect love casteth out fear.

Response: Love suffereth long, and is kind; love envieth not; love vaunteth not itself, is not puffed up.

Leader: Love never faileth. Now abideth faith, hope, love, these three; but the greatest of these is love.

Response: Greater love hath no man than this, that a man lay down his life for his friends.[52]

MALE QUARTET: *"I Shall Not Pass Again This Way"* [53]

> The bread that bringeth strength I want to give,
> The water pure that bids the thirsty live:
> I want to help the fainting day by day;
> I'm sure I shall not pass again this way.
>
> I want to give the oil of joy for tears,
> The faith to conquer crowding doubts and fears.
> Beauty for ashes may I give alway:
> I'm sure I shall not pass again this way.
>
> I want to give good measure running o'er,
> And into angry hearts I want to pour
> The answer soft that turneth wrath away;
> I'm sure I shall not pass again this way.
>
> I want to give to others hope and faith,
> I want to do all that the Master saith;
> I want to live aright from day to day;
> I'm sure I shall not pass again this way.
> —AUTHOR UNKNOWN.

STORY:

"DURER'S 'PRAYING HANDS.'" [54]

ALBRECHT DURER, the son of a Hungarian goldsmith, was born at Nuremberg, Germany, in 1471. From the time he was a wee lad he wanted to paint and draw. His gifts along this line were soon discovered, but because there were so many in his father's family and because money was so scarce, he was obliged to follow his father's trade.

Later on the opportunity to study art in a neighboring city came. During these days of study and strain he chanced to meet another struggling art student, one somewhat older than himself. They became roommates and fast friends. One day, when the battle to earn food and to meet their physical needs was seemingly going against them, Albert's friend made this suggestion: "This way of working and trying to study is intolerable. Neither of us is making a living, nor are we mastering our art. Let one of us make the living while the other continues to study. Then when the paintings begin to sell, the one who has worked may have his chance."

"Fine," replied Albert; "then, I will be the first one to work."

"I am older," said his friend, "and have not as much talent as you. You must not waste your years. Besides, I already have a job in a restaurant."

Because of his insistence, Albert agreed to the new arrangement. He went to the studio the next day with renewed zeal and with great joy, working faithfully to master his art, spending long hours in painstaking study and practice. The older man served tables, washed dishes, scrubbed floors, and did any odd jobs he could find, in order to have money enough to buy food and to pay rent. He worked from early in the morning until late at night, but he did it cheerfully, for he knew that he was helping his young friend; then, too, he looked forward to the day when he could again take up his study of art.

At last the day came when Albert made his first sale, a wood carving. He rushed home with the money and dropped it, making it jingle on the table. It was the living-room, dining-room, and kitchen table, for they occupied but one room. The money was enough to buy their food and pay their rent for many weeks ahead.

"Now, I'll be the breadwinner," he said with glee, "and you can go back to the studio tomorrow. By the time this money is gone, surely there will be another sale."

The older friend left his work in the restaurant and again took up his brush. He spent long hours, working with eagerness and high anticipation, yet he made slow progress. His fingers were stiff, his muscles knotted, and his knuckles so enlarged that the work was cumbersome.

Albert encouraged him as best he could, yet they both came to see that something had happened to his hands during the days and weeks he had slaved so tirelessly. The work had stiffened the muscles, enlarged the joints, and twisted the fingers until he could no longer handle his brush with mastery and skill. Gradually the older friend came to realize that his art would have to be sacrificed forever and that he would have to return to his work in the restaurant.

Albert was heartbroken when he realized what had happened to his friend. He would always care for him and be eternally grateful to him, but he could not give back the suppleness to his fingers that was necessary for his work. One day he returned unexpectedly to his room and heard the voice of his friend raised in prayer. As he stood quietly by the door, he saw those work-worn hands raised in prayer and heard his friend praying for his success, asking God to give to young Albert the skill he had once dreamed that he himself might possess. A great emotion swept over Albert, as he said to himself: "I can never give back the lost skill to those hands, but I can show to the world the feeling of love and gratitude which is mine for his noble deed. I will paint his hands as I see them now, and it may be that when people look at the picture, they, too, will appreciate what he has done. Perhaps some day the world will know of my deep gratitude for this beautiful, unselfish service."

PRAYER:

Teach us, good Lord, to serve Thee as Thou deservest; to give and not to count the cost; to fight and not to heed the wounds; to toil and not to seek for rest, nor for any reward save knowing that we do Thy will: through Jesus Christ our Lord. AMEN.[55]

POEM: *"The Touch of Human Hands"* [56]

> The touch of human hands—
> That is the boon we ask;
> For groping, day by day,
> Along the stony way,
> We need the comrade heart
>   That understands,
> And the warmth, the living warmth
>   Of human hands.

The touch of human hands—
Not vain, unthinking words,
Nor that cold charity
Which shuns our misery;
We seek a loyal friend
 Who understands,
And the warmth, the pulsing warmth
 Of human hands.

The touch of human hands—
Such care as was in him
Who walked in Galilee
Beside the silver sea;
We need a patient guide
 Who understands,
And the warmth, the living warmth
 Of human hands.

—THOMAS CURTIS CLARK.

BENEDICTION:

May the grace of Christ our Saviour
 And the Father's boundless love,
With the Holy Spirit's favor,
 Rest upon us from above.

—JOHN NEWTON.

GROUP V

Interpretations of Pictures, Poems, and Hymns

SERVICE XIX: TO EACH HIS TASK

AIM: To uphold in the thinking of the group the challenge of Jesus as it comes to the youth of today.

INSTRUMENTAL PRELUDE: Air for the G String (J. S. BACH).

CALL TO WORSHIP:

> God be merciful to us, and bless us,
> And cause His face to shine upon us;
> That Thy way may be known upon earth,
> And Thy salvation unto all nations.
>
> O worship the Lord in the beauty of holiness!
> Fear before Him all the earth.

HYMN: "Great Master, Touch Us With Thy Skillful Hand."
(Words read by leader while music is played softly.)

Response (to be sung by group):

> Thou who taught the thronging people
>   By blue Galilee;
> Speak to us, Thy erring children,
>   Teach us purity.
>
> Thou whose touch could heal the leper,
>   Make the blind to see;
> Touch our hearts and turn the sinning
>   Into purity.
>
> Thou whose word could still the tempest,
>   Calm the raging sea;

Hush the storm of human passion,
  Give us purity.

Thou who sinless met the temper;
  Grant, O Christ, that we
May overcome the bent to evil
  By Thy purity.

—HENRY S. NINDE.

DEDICATION TO THE TASK:

Leader: Let us hear the words of Jesus as he dedicates himself to the task:

Response: The Spirit of the Lord is upon me; because he anointed me to preach good tidings to the poor. He hath sent me to proclaim release to the captives, and recovering of sight to the blind, to set at liberty them that are bruised, to proclaim the acceptable year of the Lord.

Leader: Let us hear the words of Jesus as he called his disciples:

Response: And Jesus, walking by the sea of Galilee, saw two brethren, Simon called Peter, and Andrew his brother, casting a net into the sea: for they were fishers. And he saith unto them, Follow me, and I will make you fishers of men. And they straightway left their nets, and followed him. And going on from thence, he saw two other brethren, James the son of Zebedee, and John his brother, in a ship with Zebedee their father, mending their nets; and he called them. And they left the ship and their father, and followed him.

Leader: Let us hear the words of Jesus as he calls us to follow him:

Response: If any man will come after me, let him deny himself, and take up his cross, and follow me. For whosoever will save his life shall lose it: but whosoever shall lose his life for my sake, the same shall save it.[57]

Dedication:

O thou who dost the vision send,
  And gives to each his task,
And with the task sufficient strength,
  Show us Thy will, we ask;
Give us a conscience bold and good,
  Give us a purpose true,
That it may be our highest joy
  Our Father's work to do.

> O Jesus, Prince of life and truth,
>   Beneath Thy banner bright,
> We dedicate our strength and youth
>   To battle for the right;
> We give our lives with glad intent
>   To serve the world and Thee,
> To die, to suffer and be spent
>   To set our brothers free.[58]

—JOHN E. BODE.

STORY:

AN INTERPRETATION OF ZIMMERMANN'S "CHRIST AND THE FISHERMAN." [59]

IF WE would understand the attraction of Christ, his sympathy, kindliness, and understanding, let us search for the message of this picture. He is not shown here as a remote, kingly figure to whom persons would go with fear and trembling. Here is the Master and Friend, the Seeker after men.

The scene is near the shore of the Sea of Galilee. Jesus was passing along this way and saw the stalwart young men with their father in the fishing boat. Something in their faces, something in their conduct, or some chance word they spoke may have told him that these young men would be useful to him as helpers in the work of the Kingdom. Immediately he spoke to them and, attracted by his wonderful personality, they left their boats. They could not desert their father, and so there by the shore Jesus talked with the three; Zebedee, the father, and James and John, the young men. The fishing boat is left with a servant or companion who has not heeded the call of Jesus. Zebedee brought some of the fishing nets along, no doubt thinking it would be a good time to mend them while the young Teacher would be talking to his sons.

As we look at the group to whom Jesus is talking, we are attracted by the figure of the sturdy fisherman. He has forgotten that the nets need mending, and leans eagerly toward Jesus with a look of deep yearning to understand. Jesus is bent toward him; and as if to help make the contact more real, he holds the toil-worn hand of the old man with both of his. Perhaps he is trying to make him understand his purposes for a spiritual Kingdom, in which he will use many followers.

As we look at the two young men, we recognize John as the one nearest to Jesus, looking intently at him with reverent eyes, eager to understand all that this marvelous teacher is telling him. The artist shows that he does not fully understand the meaning of this call to service, for he has put him partly in the shadow. The light coming from Jesus touches his eyes and shows that he will continue to inquire the way. James seems to be very slow to grasp the meaning of Jesus' words. His face is still further in the shadow.

In contrast to the three men, let us look at the face and figure of Christ. We can realize the attraction of his personality as we see him here. There is something majestic in the calm authority of his face and figure which makes us sure that we could safely follow where he leads. Could any one doubt his ability to lead to a victorious way of life? All down through the ages the call of Christ has come to young men and young women to consecrate themselves to his way of life, and to service in his Kingdom. Not all of us can immediately understand the call or even the purposes of his Kingdom. Like James and John, we may declare our loyalty to him and learn his words and ways, with assurance that some day there will be work for us to do in his Kingdom.

HYMN: *"Take Thou Our Minds, Dear Lord."*

PRAYER:

O Thou Master of all men, we have heard Thy voice as it has called us to forsake all and follow Thee. We have promised to serve Thee, but ofttimes we have allowed the desire of the moment or the pull of the crowd to keep us from our high resolves. Forgive us for the things we have done which we ought not to have done; forgive us also for the things we have left undone which we should have done. We thank Thee that Thou hast given us a place in the work of Thy Kingdom. Grant unto us a vision of the things we can do to speed the coming of Thy Kingdom in this world. Teach us to be patient as we work in companionship with Thee. Show us how to win the indifferent ones, and how to turn the straying ones back to Thee. Forbid that we should ever hide the light as it comes from Thee; forbid that we should ever be a stumblingblock to any who are searching the way, but may we lift Thee up in our lives until all men are drawn unto Thee. In the name of Jesus, we pray. AMEN.

HYMN: *"Are Ye Able?"*

POSTLUDE: Music to hymn tune *"Arthur's Seat."*

GROUP V

Interpretations of Pictures, Poems, and Hymns

SERVICE XX: THE TOUCH OF JOY

Aim: To lead to a greater desire to help others to find joy in life.

Instrumental Prelude: *"Hymn to Joy"* (Beethoven).

Call to Worship:

> O be joyful in the Lord, all ye lands:
> Serve the Lord with gladness,
> And come before his presence with a song.
>
> O go your way into his gates with thanksgiving,
> And into his courts with praise:
> Be thankful unto him,
> And speak good of his name.
> For the Lord is gracious,
> His mercy is everlasting:
> And his truth endureth from generation to
>   generation.

Hymn: *"Joyful, Joyful, We Adore Thee,"* or
"I Thank Thee, Lord, for Life."

Responsive Reading:

Leader: God be merciful unto us, and bless us; and cause his face to shine upon us; that thy way may be known upon earth, thy saving health among all nations.

Response: Let all the people praise thee, O God; let all the people praise thee.

Leader: O let the nations be glad and sing for joy: for thou shalt judge the people righteously, and govern the nations upon earth.

Response: Let the people praise thee, O God; let all the people praise thee.

Leader: Then shall the earth yield her increase; and God, even our own God, shall bless us.

Response: Let the people praise thee, O God; let all the people praise thee.

Leader: Make a joyful noise unto the Lord, all ye lands. Serve the Lord with gladness: come before his presence with singing.

Response: Let the people praise thee, O God; let all the people praise thee.[60]

"SALUTATION OF THE DAWN"

> Listen to the Exhortation of the Dawn!
> Look to this Day!
> For it is Life, and the very Life of Life.
> In its brief course lie all the
> Verities and Realities of your Existence;
> The Bliss of Growth,
> The Glory of Action,
> The Splendor of Beauty;
> For Yesterday is but a Dream,
> And Tomorrow is only a Vision;
> But Today well lived makes
> Every yesterday a Dream of Happiness,
> And every Tomorrow a Vision of Hope.
> Look well therefore to this Day!
> Such is the Salutation of the Dawn."[61]

> —FROM THE SANSKRIT.

HYMN: *"Rejoice, Ye Pure in Heart."*

STORY:

"PIPPA PASSES" [62]

PIPPA LIVED in the great factory town of Asolo, noted for its many mills. This beautiful old city was set in the midst of a picturesque valley, with a river running between the hills. The people were very proud of these factories, where great bolts of silk and hundreds of spools of thread were made and sent to many parts of the world.

Pippa had been working in one of the factories for some time, earning barely enough to supply her meager wants; but she was happy and contented in her work, for she enjoyed watching the bright colors as she wound the thread, coil over coil, on the spools. The work was seldom monotonous, for she found diversion in thinking of the great people who would wear this silk. When she saw a lovely lady on the streets, dressed in the silk she had made, Pippa would say to herself, "I am glad that I had a part in making you beautiful."

There was one day in the entire year that Pippa called her own. She was glad when the Sabbath came, for she liked to go to the dimly lighted church and join in singing the hymns—but that was God's day. Her day, however, came in the summer when the days were the longest, the flowers the brightest, and the songs of the birds the sweetest.

Pippa loved the beautiful old city, but she always spent her day in the country. She did not mind the walk, for there were so many interesting things to see. On this, her day, when she awoke and saw the bright sunshine, her heart was filled with joy and she sang her happiest song:

> "The year's at the spring,
> And day's at the morn;
> Morning's at seven;
> The hillside's dew-pearled;
> The lark's on the wing,
> The snail's on the thorn,
> God's in His heaven—
> All's right with the world."

Her day, as compared to the rest of the year, was only a mite of a twelve-hour treasure; but, somehow, she managed to crowd enough happiness into it to lighten her days of toil, and to brighten all the other days of the year. On this day there was no limit to the possibilities, for in her imagination she could act out her fondest dreams— she could be anything she wished. Usually she chose to be a beautiful lady, living in a great house, with many lovers coming to woo her.

"Today I will not be Pippa who winds the silk; I'm going to act out fancy's fullest dream. I'm going to be, in turn, each of Asolo's four happiest persons."

First she imagines herself the wife of Luca, the owner of the mills, living in the magnificent house on the hillside, and enjoying all the luxury that wealth can bestow. To make her dream more real, she walks by the great house, lingers to gaze at the flowers in the garden, and sings her song under the great lady's window. Pippa does not know of the sorrow in the great house and of the tragedy that was being enacted at that very moment. Luca has just been murdered by his wife's lover. But when the unfaithful wife heard Pippa singing,

"God's in His Heaven,"

she became disgusted with her own weakness, and in remorse dismissed her secret lover.

Then Pippa thinks of the couple that is to be married in the church at noon that day. As she runs along the hillside, she decides that she will be the bride. She muses on the beautiful clothes, the loveliness of the bride, and the words of love that will be whispered to her. She says to herself: "But sometimes lovers grow cold, and men come to hate their wives. No, I will not be the bride. I will be Luigi. Each evening I see him walking with his mother and he seems to be so happy and contented. Surely his cup of joy has been pressed down and running over. God must be pleased to see his children enjoy his world so much." But Pippa did not know of the men who at that very moment were plotting against the life of Luigi.

As Pippa ran along singing her happy song, she passed the studio of an artist who painted wonderful pictures; but today he could think of nothing to paint. He heard Pippa's song and hurried to the door, only to catch a glimpse of her; but he saw the very picture that he had been wanting. He painted her hastily, just as he saw her—with her hat tied by the streamers, her face turned toward the sky, and her hair shining in the sun. She furnished him the inspiration that he needed, and when the picture was finished it was his masterpiece.

Pippa then passes a vagabond who was discouraged; life had lost all attraction for him. He had played with the world and had found it too rough for him. He was defeated and disillusioned; but as he listened to Pippa's cheerful song, he felt that perhaps, after all, there was something worth while that he might do.

A condemned man gazing idly through the narrow window of his cell saw Pippa as she flitted by and heard her singing,

"God's in His heaven,"

and immediately sought out a priest and begged to be taught how to

— 134—

pray. His fellow-prisoners standing near by were surprised to hear the unusual words coming from his lips:

> "Father in heaven,
> Blot out my sins
> And remember them
> No more against me."

Pippa's day came to a close all too soon. She had seen many illustrious people who had accomplished much, and many whom she thought to be happy. As she thought of these people she mused within herself: "I wonder how near I'll ever come to approaching any of those fortunate people. Perhaps tomorrow as I wind the silk, I can, at least, come near enough to touch the hem of the garments that they will wear."

"O God, I did want to make some one happy today, but I did not find anyone, so I just helped myself. I hope that Thou in Thy heaven wilt understand."

Then she repeated a hymn which she often sang in church: After all, perhaps,

> "All service ranks the same with God—
> With God, whose puppets, best and worst,
> Are we; there is no last nor first."

POEM:

> If I have faltered more or less
> In my great task of happiness;
> If I have moved among my race
> And shown no glorious morning face;
> If beams from happy human eyes
> Have moved me not; if morning skies,
> Books, and my food, and summer rain
> Knocked on my sullen heart in vain—
> Lord, Thy most pointed pleasure take
> And stab my spirit broad awake.
> —ROBERT L. STEVENSON.

LITANY OF PRAISE:

Leader: For the wonder and beauty of the universe,
Response: We praise Thee, O God.

Leader: For the joy which Thy creation brings,
Response: We thank Thee, O God.
Leader: For the material gifts which Thou hast showered upon us,
Response: We thank Thee, O God.
Leader: For the health and strength that is ours,
Response: We thank Thee, O God.
Leader: For the beauty and harmony of nature,
Response: We give Thee thanks, O God.
Leader: May we learn from nature to live according to Thy laws,
Response: We humbly pray.
Leader: As we think of the beauty which Thou hast created for our enjoyment,
Response: Help us to live nobler lives.
Leader: Grant that as happiness comes to us, we may be willing to share it with others,
Response: In Jesus' name, we pray. AMEN.

BENEDICTION.

GROUP V

Interpretations of Pictures, Poems, and Hymns

SERVICE XXI: COMPARATIVE VALUES

AIM: To lead to a truer sense of values, placing human life in its proper relation to things of lesser value.

INSTRUMENTAL PRELUDE: *"Prelude in C Minor,"* Op. 28, No. 20
(CHOPIN.)

CALL TO WORSHIP (in unison):

> "Send forth, O God, Thy light and truth,
>   And let them lead me still,
> Undaunted, in the paths of right,
>   Up to Thy holy hill:
> Then to Thy altar will I spring,
>   And in my God rejoice;
> And praise shall tune the trembling string,
>   And gratitude my voice."
>
> —JOHN QUINCY ADAMS.

PRAYER:

Eternal Father, in whom we live, move, and have our being, grant unto us a sense of Thy presence. We thank Thee that Thou hast loved all Thy children, and that Thou art not willing that any should perish. Help us to hear the cries of those who suffer; keep us from wounding any heart and thus adding to the burden of the world. Help us to remember that if we would renew our strength we must wait on Thee and grant that through communion with Thee we may find strength to face courageously the problems of life. In Jesus' name we pray. AMEN.

RESPONSIVE READING:[63]

Leader: Give not that which is holy unto the dogs, neither cast ye your pearls before swine, lest they trample them under their feet, and turn again and rend you.

Response: Therefore I say unto you, Take no thought for your life, what ye shall eat, or what ye shall drink; nor yet for your body, what ye shall put on.

Leader: Is not the life more than meat, and the body than raiment?

Response: Behold the fowls of the air: for they sow not, neither do they reap, nor gather into barns; yet your heavenly father feedeth them.

Leader: Are ye not much better than they?

Response: For after all these things do the Gentiles seek. But seek ye first the kingdom of God, and his righteousness; and all these things shall be added unto you.

HYMN: *"Love Thyself Last."*

STORY:

"THE GIFT OF TRITEMIUS" [64]

TRITEMIUS, the good abbot of the monastery, knelt before the altar in prayer. He was a great and goodly soul and every day he spent much time within the chapel praying for his own soul and the needs of the world.

As he was praying he heard from without the chapel a voice which seemed to him the saddest sound he had ever heard. He paused in prayer and, being a merciful man as well as pious, rose from his knees, crossed the chapel, and looked through the casement window to see if he could be of help to a soul in such distress. From the ground below an old woman in tattered garments and streaming gray hair looked toward the window; and, as the figure of the Abbot appeared, she reached forth her withered hands to him and cried: "Alms! Alms! For the dear love of him who gave his life for ours, save my child from bondage. My beautiful, brave first-born, chained with the slaves!"

The heart of the good Tritemius was filled with tenderness. "I can give you my prayers," he said; "perchance they will set him free."

The woman, weary and worn from her grief, but bold because of her fear for her son, cried out: "O man of God, I must have more than prayers. I must have gold to pay as ransom for my son. Perchance even as I tell you my first-born is dying. For the love of him who gave his life for ours, Alms! Alms!"

"Mother," said the Abbot, full of loving sympathy for her, "no one has ever come to our door hungry and gone away unfed. So we are always poor. We keep not a single penny for ourselves and there is not now one golden coin within our treasury. We can give you but our prayers. What more could we give?"

The woman ceased her sobbing and wailing, and in a broken voice said: "Do not mock me. I ask not for prayers, but for gold. Words will not serve me. Give me the silver candlesticks on either side of the great crucifix. God can spare them to release a soul from bondage, and perhaps in their place he will give you golden ones instead."

Tritemius stood with bated breath. How could he give as alms the candlesticks which stood at either side of the great crucifix? But as he paused there passed before his vision the figure of a lad chained as a slave.

Slowly Tritemius moved toward the altar and with trembling hands removed the silver candlesticks. Turning to the woman he said, "It shall be even as you have asked. The Lord Jesus, who loves mercy more than sacrifice, and loves all his children alike, will forgive me if I have thought more of a single soul than of these gifts piled upon his altar." Placing the gift within her upstretched hands he said: "Take what you asked and redeem your child."

With eyes filled with tears and a voice too broken to speak, the woman vanished down the pathway to set her first-born free.

It was with a heavy heart that the good Abbot knelt before the altar and prayed, this time for his own forgiveness.

All day he knelt in silent prayer until the twilight came. The last red rays of the setting sun streamed through the chapel windows. The room was flooded with light and aflame with the golden glow of sunset. It was as if the very Christ himself were there. The good Abbot raised his head from prayer, felt the presence of the Christ, and, full of grateful wonder, beheld upon the altar two candlesticks of gold.

POEM: *"O Heart"* [65]

O Heart, that beats with every human heart,
O Heart, that weeps with every human tear,
O Heart, that sings with every human song,
Fill our slow hearts with flood-tides of Thy love;

That they may beat with every human heart,
That they may weep with every human tear,
That they may sing with every human song,
And thus, through Thee, unite with all mankind.
—MAURICE ROWNTREE.

PRAYER:

Our Father, we give Thee thanks for all Thy goodness to us. We thank Thee for all the blessings of life which Thou hast so freely given. Help us to show our praise by living according to the best we know. Give unto us a better understanding of the sacredness of human life and the worth of personality. Grant that we may have a proper reverence for sacred things, and in all our dealings with others may we have the spirit of the Master. Fill our hearts with feelings of love, kindness, and consideration, and grant that we may be comrades to those who bear burdens too heavy for their strength. Help us to place a proper evaluation upon human life, putting other things of lesser value in their rightful place. This we ask in the name of the Master of all life. AMEN.

HYMN: *"O Brother Man, Fold to Thy Heart"*

O brother man, fold to thy heart thy brother!
    Where pity dwells, the peace of God is there;
To worship rightly is to love each other,
    Each smile a hymn, each kindly deed a prayer.

For he whom Jesus loved hath truly spoken:
    The holier worship which He deigns to bless
Restores the lost, and binds the spirit broken,
    And feeds the widow and the fatherless.

Follow with reverent steps the great example
    Of Him whose holy work was doing good;
So shall the wide earth seem our Father's temple,
    Each loving life a psalm of gratitude.
—JOHN G. WHITTIER.

BENEDICTION:

Now unto him that is able to keep you from falling, and to present you faultless before the presence of his glory with exceeding joy, to the only wise God our Saviour, be glory and majesty, dominion and power, both now and ever. AMEN.

GROUP V

Interpretations of Pictures, Poems, and Hymns

SERVICE XXII: A MIGHTY FORTRESS

AIM: To lead to a clearer understanding of the meaning of the hymn, "A Mighty Fortress Is Our God," and to a realization of the strength that comes from God in time of need.

INSTRUMENTAL PRELUDE: *"Romance in G"* (BEETHOVEN).

CALL TO WORSHIP:

> O come, let us sing unto the Lord,
> For the Lord is a great God,
> And a great King above all gods.
> The Lord reigneth,
> He is clothed with majesty;
> Let us come before his presence with thanksgiving,
> And into his courts with praise.

HYMN: *"Honor and Glory, Power and Salvation"*

> Honor and glory, power and salvation
> Be in the highest unto Him who reigneth.
> Changeless in heaven, over earthly changes,
>   God, the eternal.
>
> Bow down before Him, people and nations,
> See ye His glory, clearly now appearing.
> Come ye and worship Him, God in the highest,
>   Ruler forever.

INVOCATION:

Blessed be Thou, Lord God of Israel, our Father. Thine, O Lord, is the greatness, and the power, and the glory, and the victory, and the majesty; for all that is in heaven and in the earth is Thine; Thine is the kingdom, O Lord, and Thou art exalted as above all. Thy power is marvelous. In the reverence due Thy greatness, we thank Thee, and praise Thy holy name. AMEN.[66]

HYMN: *"Faith of Our Fathers."*

SCRIPTURE READING:

> God is our refuge and strength,
> A very present help in trouble.
> Therefore will we not fear, though the earth do change,
> And though the mountains be shaken into the heart of the
>   seas;
> Though the waters thereof roar and be troubled,
> Though the mountains tremble with the swelling thereof.
> The Lord of hosts is with us;
> The God of Jacob is our refuge.[67]

STORY: Interpretation of Hymn:

"A MIGHTY FORTRESS"

IT WAS Arthur C. McGiffert who said: "Great men need not that we praise them; the need is ours that we know them." [68] And we might add, that we might know their works as well.

The world is richer because Martin Luther (1483-1546) lived, yet few think of him as other than the great Reformer who gave to the German-speaking people the Bible in their own language. Seldom is he thought of as a musician, but it is through his hymns and arrangements of Psalms for singing that we gain some idea of Luther as a man.

This hymn, "A Mighty Fortress Is Our God," one of the world's masterpieces, is characteristic of the man himself. It is rugged and majestic, and expresses a confident trust in God. Carlyle said of it: "There is something in it like the sound of Alpine avalanches or the first murmur of earthquakes." Four hundred years of constant use have only served to deepen the appreciation for this hymn.

Many hymns have been written which express courage, but this one is matchless in its rugged strength, and in its note of defiance to earthly powers and firm reliance upon the supreme power of God.

It was written at a time when the people needed greater confidence and courage, and it probably accomplished as much for the Reformation as did the translation of the Bible. It was, indeed, the trumpet blast of the Reformation.

The power of this hymn lies in the fact that it expresses a firm belief that God's followers are invincible and His cause will ultimately triumph. Soon after it was written it was sung in all the churches of Saxony. It was a source of comfort to the Huguenots of France; it gave courage to the Protestant emigrants on their way to exile, and to martyrs at their death. Its popularity has increased with the years until it has become the National Hymn of Protestant Germany, and is as dear to the heart of many Germans today as is "The Fatherland" itself.

Perhaps this hymn has not been fully appreciated in America, though many Christians are beginning to realize from it the heritage which is theirs. Its popularity has increased steadily, however, since at Princeton University on the four hundredth anniversary of Luther's birth a great male chorus sang it with telling effect.

This hymn has been used under many conditions. Some years ago a terrible accident occurred in a coal mine near Scranton, Pennsylvania, where several men were buried for days, and all rescue efforts proved unsuccessful.[69] The majority of the miners were Germans. Sympathy for the wives and children of the buried men, and despair at their thwarted efforts, had created a state of nervous tension.

On the third day after the accident the excitement had grown to fever pitch. The group assembled at the mouth of the mine was ready for mob violence. A bystander cried: "It is folly to dig further; the men are not alive." A sullen murmur arose. Soon there were cries of rage against the mine owners who were not in any way responsible for the accident. Onlookers felt the tenseness of the situation; they feared a hasty word might produce an outbreak of fury.

Standing nearby was a little German girl, perhaps eleven years of age. Her pale face and frightened glances showed that she realized the danger of the moment. Suddenly with a great effort she began to sing in a hoarse whisper which could scarcely be heard:

"A mighty fortress is our God,
A bulwark never failing."

Then she gained courage and her sweet childish voice rang out in words familiar to every German from his cradle:

"Our helper He, amid the flood
Of mortal ills prevailing."

There was a silence like death. Then one voice after another joined the child's until from the entire group rose the triumphant chorus:

"Did we in our own strength confide,
Our striving would be losing;
Were not the right man on our side,
The man of God's own choosing:
Dost ask who that may be?
Christ Jesus, it is He;
Lord Sabaoth, His name,
From age to age the same,
And He must win the battle.

A solemn hush fell upon the people. The men with one accord resumed their work, and before morning the joyful cry arose from the pit that the men had been found alive.

POEM:

God is my strong salvation:
What foe have I to fear?
In darkness and temptation,
My light, my help is near.
Though hosts encamp around me,
Firm in the fight I stand;
What terror can confound me
With God at my right hand?
—JAMES MONTGOMERY.

PRAYER:

Almighty God, Thou who art the source of all our strength, Life of our life, and Father of us all, pour out Thy spirit upon us. O Thou for whom our hearts are made, whose comradeship we crave, forgive the dullness of our vision. Forgive us for our slowness to obey Thy divine commands. Quicken our hearts and give us a fresh devotion to Thee. As we think of that mighty army of prophets and martyrs who suffered that Thy cause may be upheld, we thank Thee for their courage. Their example makes us ashamed of our lack of faith. We are indeed grateful for this heritage which has come to us. Make us more worthy to pass on Thy message to those who come after us. Increase our faith and grant unto us the strength to live the victorious life. In Christ's name we pray. AMEN.

HYMN: *"Life of Ages, Richly Poured"*

Life of ages, richly poured,
   Love of God, unspent and free,
Flowing in the prophet's word
   And the people's liberty.

Never was to chosen race
   That unstinted tide confined:
Thine is every time and place,
   Fountain sweet of heart and mind;

Breathing in the thinker's creed,
   Pulsing in the hero's blood;
Nerving simplest thought and deed;
   Freshening time with truth and good;

Consecrating art and song,
   Holy book and pilgrim track;
Hurling floods of tyrant wrong
   From the sacred limits back.
        —SAMUEL JOHNSON.

BENEDICTION.

Interpretations of Pictures, Poems, and Hymns

SERVICE XXIII: FAIREST LORD JESUS

Aim: To lift up in the thinking of the group the meaning of the hymn, "Fairest Lord Jesus," that it may be sung with understanding, and may lead to a greater devotion to Jesus.

Instrumental Prelude: *"Passion Chorale"* (Harmonized by J. S. Bach).[70]

Call to Worship:

> Oh give thanks unto the Lord,
> Call upon his name;
> Make known among the people his doing;
> Sing unto him, sing praises unto him;
> Talk ye of all his marvelous works.
>
> The earth is the Lord's, and the fullness thereof;
> The world, and they that dwell therein.
> O worship the Lord in the beauty of holiness:
> Fear before Him all the earth.

Hymn: *"Holy, Holy, Holy, Lord God Almighty,"* or *"The Spacious Firmament on High."*

Scripture Reading (in unison):

> The Lord reigneth, he is clothed with majesty;
> The Lord is clothed with strength,
> Wherewith he hath girded himself;
> The world also is established, that it cannot be moved.
> Thy throne is established of old:

Thou art from everlasting.
The floods have lifted up, O Lord,
The floods have lifted up their voices;
The Lord on high is mightier than the noise of many waters,
Yea, than the mighty waves of the sea.[71]

STORY: Interpretation of the Hymn,

"FAIREST LORD JESUS"

IN SPITE of the proof that the Crusaders never used this hymn, it has been known throughout the ages as the Crusader's Hymn. Written in 1677, it could not have been used by the Crusaders; but it was, no doubt, sung by the German pilgrims as they marched toward Jerusalem. Others have called it "The Marching Song of the Out-of-doors." While it is essentially a nature hymn, it is more than that. It is a hymn of royalty, in which the writer is striving to express his adoration and devotion to a supreme Being.

We like to think of this hymn as the Crusader's Hymn, because it reminds us of those stalwart Knights in the courts of Europe. Let us visualize these Crusaders, fired with enthusiasm for the cause which has gripped them, erect upon their horses, and ready to ride forth in the service of their King. How eager they are to leave these courts, with the man-made splendor, and engage in a hazardous conquest for the glory of their earthly King! How courageously they face danger, and how zealously they enter into the conquest!

As they ride across the continent there is much of beauty to be seen. They often stand in awe in the presence of a wonderful work of nature; and, no doubt, they are often constrained to worship their Creator because the beauty about them has struck a responsive chord. Let us stand with them on the top of a mountain and compare, as they do, the beauty of nature with the Ruler of all nature. Soon we shall realize, as they did, that, although meadows and woodlands are beautiful, especially when arrayed in the garb of spring, God is fairer and purer than all this physical appearance of beauty. And we begin to realize that this Divine Personality does change human personality and make the woeful heart to sing.

Let us contrast the Christian of today with the Crusaders. The cause which the Christian serves is far greater, and the Ruler to whom he gives allegiance is the Creator, not only of all nature, but of earthly kings as well. How does the mental attitude of the Christian compare with that of the Knights of old? As he enlists in the cause of Jesus, and stands in the court of God, does he, with head erect and with a heart full of adoration, sing praise to the Creator and Ruler of all nature? Does he go forth as joyously and courageously; does he serve as zealously as did the Knights in the days of old? As he accepts the challenge of Christ, does he honor, cherish, and worship the Ruler of all nature?

The tune for this hymn has been arranged from a Silesian folk song. No one knows how far into the past it reaches. It has been sung by all classes of people from the humblest shepherd to the highest dignitary of the land. On one occasion a musician heard some haymakers singing this tune toward the close of their day's work and was impressed with the beauty of it. He felt that it should be recorded in order that it might be shared with others. This he did and it appeared in 1842 for the first time in a collection of folk songs. About eight years later it was arranged as a hymn tune by Professor Richard Storrs Willis (1819-1900) and published for the first time in America.

As we sing this hymn, let us think of Christ at the age of twelve, as Hofmann has pictured him, on the occasion of his visit to the temple. Here we see him talking with the doctors and lawyers and other learned men. He is truly a fair Jesus, with all the ideal beauty which artists have attributed to him through the ages.[72]

RESPONSIVE READING:

Leader: One thing I asked of the Lord, that will I seek after: That I may behold the beauty of the Lord.

Response (to be sung):

Fairest Lord Jesus,
Ruler of all nature,
O Thou of God and man the Son,
Thee will I cherish,
Thee will I honor,
Thee, my soul's Glory, Joy, and Crown.

Leader: He is altogether lovely.

Response: Fair are the meadows,
Fairer still the woodlands,
Robed in the blooming garb of spring:
Jesus is fairer,

Jesus is purer,
Who makes the woeful heart to sing.

Leader: The Lord will arise upon thee,
And his glory shall be seen upon thee.

Response: Fair is the sunshine,
Fairer still the moonlight,
And all the twinkling starry host:
Jesus shines brighter,
Jesus shines purer
Than all the angels heaven can boast.

Leader: And nations shall come to thy light,
And kings to the brightness of thy rising.

Response: All fairest beauty,
Heavenly and earthly,
Wondrously, Jesus, is found in thee:
None can be nearer,
Fairer or dearer
Than thou, my Saviour, art to me.

Leader: O Lord, how excellent is thy name in all the earth.

Response: Beautiful Saviour;
Lord of the nations;
Son of God and Son of man.
Glory and honor,
Praise, adoration,
Now and evermore be thine.

Poem: *"Young and Radiant, He Is Standing"* [78]

Young and radiant, he is standing
As he stood at Salem's shrine;
Just a lad, a lad forever,
With a look and grace divine!
"Tell me, how it is ye sought me?
Wist ye not my Father's plan?
I must be about his business,
Would I be a Son of Man."

I can see him humbly kneeling,
As he knelt upon the hill;

> While the waters hushed their music,
>   And the night grew bright and still:
> "Brothers, tell me why ye sought me?
>   Wist ye not my Father's plan?
> He must grow in grace and wisdom,
>   Would he be a Son of Man."
>
> —ALLEN EASTMAN CROSS.

HYMN: *"Jesus, the Very Thought of Thee"*

> Jesus, the very thought of Thee
>   With sweetness fills the breast;
> But sweeter far Thy face to see,
>   And in Thy presence rest.
>
> Nor voice can sing, nor heart can frame,
>   Nor can the memory find
> A sweeter sound than Thy blest name,
>   O Saviour of mankind!
>
> O Hope of every contrite heart,
>   O Joy of all the meek,
> To those who ask, how kind Thou art!
>   How good to those who seek!
>
> Jesus, our only joy be Thou,
>   As Thou our prize wilt be;
> Jesus, be Thou our glory now,
>   And through eternity.

PRAYER:

We thank Thee, our Father, for Thy thoughtfulness in making the world so wondrously fair. We praise Thee for the glory of the morning, the beauty of the sunset, and for all the joy which Thy creation brings. Open our eyes that we may become more sensitive to beauty in its various forms. Grant that the glories of nature may remind us of Thee, who art the Creator and Ruler of all nature. Touch our hearts that this love of nature may lead us into a greater love for Thee. In Jesus' name we pray. AMEN.

BENEDICTION:

Now unto the King eternal, immortal, invisible, the only wise God, be honor and glory forever and ever. AMEN.

GROUP VI

Special Occasions

MISSIONS

SERVICE XXIV: FROM PHILOSOPHY TO THE JUNGLES

AIM: To lift up in the thinking of the group the responsibility of each one for helping to carry Christ's message around the world.

INSTRUMENTAL PRELUDE: Chorale from *"Sleepers Awake"* (BACH).

CALL TO WORSHIP:

Leader: Arise, shine; for thy light is come, and the glory of the Lord is risen upon thee.

Response: How beautiful upon the mountains are the feet of him that bringeth good tidings, that publisheth peace; that saith unto Zion, Thy God reigneth!

Leader: From the rising of the sun even unto the going down of the same my name shall be great among the nations, saith the Lord of hosts.

Response: The Gentiles shall come to thy light, and kings to the brightness of thy rising.

Leader: The Lord hath made known his salvation: his righteousness hath he openly showed in the sight of the nations.

Response: They shall come from the east and from the west, and from the north and from the south, and shall sit down in the kingdom of God.

INVOCATION:

Look upon us, O Lord, and let all the darkness of our souls vanish before the beams of Thy brightness. Fill us with holy love, and open to us the treasures of Thy wisdom. All our desire is known unto

Thee, wherefore perfect what Thou hast begun, and what Thy Spirit hast awakened us to ask in prayer. We seek Thy face; turn Thy face unto us, and show us Thy glory, then shall our own longing be satisfied through Jesus Christ our Lord. AMEN.[74]

Prayer Response: "Father of Lights, in Whom There Is No Shadow."

RESPONSIVE READING: [75]

Leader: Then saith he unto his disciples, The harvest truly is plenteous, but the laborers are few; pray ye therefore the Lord of the harvest, that he will send forth laborers into his harvest.

Response (to be sung):

> Fling out the banner! let it float
> Skyward and seaward, high and wide;
> The sun, that lights its shining folds,
> The cross, on which the Saviour died.

Leader: Jesus said: I am the good shepherd, and know my sheep, and am known of mine; and I lay down my life for the sheep.

Response: Fling out the banner! angels bend
> In anxious silence o'er the sign,
> And vainly seek to comprehend
> The wonder of the love divine.

Leader: And other sheep I have, which are not of this fold: them also I must bring, and they shall hear my voice; and there shall be one fold, and one shepherd.

Response: Fling out the banner! distant lands
> Shall see from far the glorious sight;
> And nations, crowding to be born,
> Baptize their spirits in its light.

Leader: Go ye therefore, and make disciples of all nations, teaching them to observe all things; and, lo, I am with you alway, even unto the end of the world.

Response: Fling out the banner! sin-sick souls,
> That sink and perish in the strife
> Shall touch in faith its radiant hem,
> And spring immortal into life.

> —GEORGE W. DOANE.

STORY:

"FROM PHILOSOPHY TO THE JUNGLES" [76]

ALBERT SCHWEITZER, an outstanding musician and scholar of Europe, has hidden himself away in the heart of Africa, ministering to the needy savages. His friends, seeing the crowds that throng Westminster Abbey to hear his organ concerts, find it difficult to understand why he insists on returning to Africa. They marvel at his skill as a musician—he is perhaps the greatest interpreter of Bach in Europe today. They try to hold him in Europe; but he gives only a few concerts to raise money for his mission, and returns to his work in Africa.

When one sees Dr. Schweitzer seated at the organ in the Abbey, the shrine that is centuries old, and hears the music as it sounds through the vaulted nave, one's thoughts go back to those builders of the past, who sought to reproduce in stone the beauty of an avenue of trees. Listening to the harmony of the organ, one is transported to the groves of Africa, where Dr. Schweitzer is striving to bring harmony and beauty to life by ministering to the natives. His decision to return to Africa is, after all, consistent with the very nature of the man himself. Playing the organ in the Abbey, healing the bodies of the natives, and bringing peace to troubled souls are fruits of a dedicated life.

Albert Schweitzer was born in 1875 at Kayserberg in Upper Alsace, that beautiful disputed country bordering on the Rhine. Soon after his birth his father was sent to Gunsbach, where he served as a Protestant minister until his death. Albert studied at the University of Strasbourg, also in Berlin and Paris, and at the early age of twenty-three was a Doctor of Philosophy. At twenty-eight he was considered the greatest authority on the construction of organs in Europe. At this time many doors were open to him. He was principal of the theological school of St. Thomas, was the author of several books, and was in demand for concerts. Why did he wish to turn his back upon the honors of the world and bury himself in the jungles of Africa?

Early in life Albert had sought to identify himself with the weak and unfortunate. He could not enjoy a good meal without thinking of those who seldom have enough to eat. He believed that one should not think of his life as belonging to himself, but that if he were spared personal pain he should help in diminishing the pain of others. Then one day an insignificant thing happened which changed the entire course of his life. While looking at the statue of a Negro by the French artist, Bartholdi, an idea came to him which he could not dismiss from his mind. The expression on the face of this Negro at the feet of Admiral Bruat carried a message which he could never forget. There was unmistakable meaning in the sadness of the eyes and the tragedy written on the features.

Louder and louder came the cry from Africa, "Come over and help us," and it was very clear to Dr. Schweitzer that he must do something about the suffering of the Negro. He decided that he had given enough of his life to science, theology, and music. Resigning from the theological school, he made preparation to enter medical school in order to fit himself for this new type of work. His friends were astonished that he should turn from the fields in which he had already gained recognition to one that promised isolation or self-exile. At the age of thirty he began his education over again—this time in the field of medicine. In the meantime his wife studied nursing, and in 1913 they sailed for, what seemed to them, the neediest corner of the world.

Dr. Schweitzer built his hospital on the Ogowe River in French Equatorial Africa. When the news of his arrival spread, natives suffering from many kinds of tropical diseases poured into Lambarene. His only assistant, in addition to his wife, was the Negro cook who also acted as interpreter. His first clinics were held out of doors and there were many obstacles to overcome. It was difficult to persuade the natives to obey orders, and dependable helpers could not be secured. However, during the first nine months of his stay, he treated over two thousand patients and performed many difficult operations.

During the World War Dr. Schweitzer was supporting himself as a medical missionary in French Territory in Africa. He was not suspected of any war activity; but being of German parentage, the order came for his arrest. He and his wife were placed under guard as prisoners of war. There were so many protests that finally they were released, only to be arrested again and taken to a prison camp in France. After many months freedom came to them through the exchange of war prisoners. Without funds and broken in health, they went to Sweden and Switzerland, where, by giving concerts, sufficient money was raised to resume their work in Africa.

Upon their return to Lambarene, Dr. Schweitzer and his wife

found that the roof of the hospital had fallen in; the entire place had overgrown with weeds, and much of the work had to be done over again. It was not long, however, until the buildings were repaired, the brush cleared, and their ministry to the Negroes was resumed.

When his funds are exhausted, Dr. Schweitzer goes to Europe and stays barely long enough to raise enough money to carry on his work. To his friends who cannot understand why he rushes back to Africa he says, "If you could be with me just one morning, and see a patient as he is brought to me in much pain. I quiet him by telling him that I am going to put him to sleep, and that when he wakes he will not feel any more pain. Then, after the operation, if you could see the happiness on the face of the Negro, and the gratitude that he tries to express, as he grasps my hand, exclaiming, "I've no more pain; I've no more pain." Then, perhaps, you would understand why I must minister to my needy brothers in Africa." And today Dr. Schweitzer is there removing tumors and treating leprosy, sleeping sickness, and other tropical diseases.

PRAYER:

Our Father, may we not be content to enjoy the good things of life without sharing with others. Reveal unto us the things we can do in bringing Thy Kingdom to the world and spreading the reign of righteousness. Those of us who cannot go to other fields to carry Thy message, may we be willing to give of our means in sending others. Grant unto each of us the grace to leave this world a fairer place than we found it. Give unto us the same heart of compassion for the needs of the world as was in the Lord, in whose name we claim Thy power. AMEN.

OFFERTORY:

Leader: Whatsoever ye do, do it heartily, as to the Lord, and not unto men.

Response: We could give Thee nothing, O Thou great Giver of every perfect gift, if Thou hadst not first given it to us. Grant that this cause to which we are devoted may prosper under Thy guidance. Give us the grace to consecrate not only our possessions, but ourselves to Thy service. May Thy kingdom come and Thy will be done on earth as it is in heaven. AMEN.

HYMN: *"Jesus Shall Reign Where'er the Sun,"* or
"Christ for the World We Sing."

BENEDICTION: Unto God's protection we commit you; the Lord mercifully with his favor look upon you, and fill you with all spiritual benedictions and grace. AMEN.

SERVICE XXV: BECOMING AWARE

AIM: To lead to a greater awareness of the needs of those about us, to drive out all influences which make for exclusiveness, and to co-operate in such a manner as will bring about the common good of all.

INSTRUMENTAL PRELUDE: Hymn Tune, *"Mozart."*

CALL TO WORSHIP:

> O Lord, all glorious, Life of life!
> To Thee we raise our grateful songs;
> Lift up our souls from thoughts of self
> To Thee, to whom all life belongs.
>
> From Thee all good desires proceed,
> All holy thoughts we gain from Thee;
> The good we do is Thine alone,
> Thine shall our heart's thanksgiving be.

HYMN: *"The Voice of God Is Calling."*

RESPONSIVE READING:

Leader: But when he saw the multitudes, he was moved with compassion on them, because they fainted, and were scattered abroad, as sheep having no shepherd.

Response (to be sung):

> Master, no offering costly and sweet
> May we, like Magdalene, lay at thy feet;

Yet may love's incense rise, sweeter than sacrifice,
Dear Lord, to thee, dear Lord, to thee.

Leader: And whosoever shall give to drink unto one of these little
ones a cup of cold water only in the name of a disciple, verily I
say unto you, he shall in no wise lose his reward.

Response: Daily our lives would show weakness made strong,
Toilsome and gloomy ways brightened with song;
Some deeds of kindness done, some souls by patience
won,
Dear Lord, to thee, dear Lord, to thee.

Leader: Pure religion and undefiled before God and the Father is this,
To visit the fatherless and widows in their affliction, and to keep
himself unspotted from the world.

Response: Some word of hope for hearts burdened with fears,
Some balm of peace for eyes blinded with tears,
Some dews of mercy shed, some wayward footsteps led,
Dear Lord, to thee, dear Lord, to thee.

Leader: And thou shalt love the Lord thy God with all thy heart, and
all thy soul, and with all thy mind, and with all thy strength.
And thou shalt love thy neighbor as thyself.[77]

Response: Thus, in thy service, Lord, till eventide
Closes the day of life, may we abide.
And when earth's labors cease, let us depart in peace,
Dear Lord, to thee, dear Lord, to thee.

HYMN: *"This Is My Father's World,"* or
"There's a Wideness in God's Mercy."

STORY:

"A MODERN MATRIARCH" [78]

BORN in 1875 of parents who had formerly been slaves, Mary Bethune
grew up in an out-of-the-way community in South Carolina. Her
mother was the direct descendant of a ruling family in West Africa,
where even today descent, kinship, and succession are reckoned through
the mother. Like the ancient matriarchs of primitive Africa, Mary had
a great desire to lead and direct. Her earliest years, however, were
not different from those of other poor colored children in the vicinity
of Maysville, a country town in the midst of vast, uninviting acres of
swampy rice land.

Mary's first opportunity came when she was permitted to attend a mission school for Negro girls which was opened four miles from her home. Her record in this school was such that she was awarded a scholarship at Scotia Seminary, a school maintained by the Presbyterian Church at Concord, N. C. This scholarship was made possible by a woman of South Denver, Colorado, who, in all probability, had little idea that her gift would prove to be so far-reaching.

No one prepared Mary for the experiences ahead, and she knew little of what to expect in a boarding school. But with high hopes, she set off for school, dressed in her best and wearing a tag to indicate her destination. The styles of Maysville had not added to her personal appearance, and for some time she afforded a great deal of amusement to the students of Scotia, but she hid her sensitiveness behind her own contagious laugh and busied herself with her studies.

Here at Scotia Mary made her first plans for her life's work. At this time she had no thought of serving her own people in America, but instead she wanted to go to Africa as a missionary. Her great love of Africa had come through her mother, in whose heart the drums of her native country had beaten during the weary years of slavery. As a further preparation for special work Mary attended Moody Bible Institute for two years; but when she applied to one of the Mission Boards for work in Africa, she was told that there was no station available. This was a great disappointment, but gradually she came to see that there were opportunities at home as well as abroad.

On a visit to Tuskegee Institute, where she saw for the first time the great institution which Booker T. Washington had built, there came to her a vision of a similar institution which would provide education for Negro women, and over which a woman would preside. In it there would be taught all the essentials of homemaking, but with no neglect of citizenship. Surely the time was ripe for launching such a project.

But Mary's vision was not realized until 1904, when she moved to Daytona, Florida, and opened a school in a small dwelling house. She had very little money, so she furnished her school with pieces of furniture which she collected from some interested persons. Empty soap boxes served for desks and chairs. Then she gathered five wide-eyed, dark-skinned little girls and the Daytona Normal and Industrial School began. She taught them to read, write, and sing, and to be neat and industrious.

There were many difficulties in the way, but Mrs. Bethune persevered. She was married, but she did not allow the claims of her home to crowd out her desire to help her own people. One day she invited some people of the city to visit her school. They listened as the girls gave their recitations and sang from the front porch. Realizing the importance of the work she was doing, they decided to form an organization to help her. Even with their help, there were times when her need was great. Gradually more people became interested in the school until it grew to an enrollment of over 400 pupils and a faculty of more than thirty teachers.

Mrs. Bethune has undertaken many projects, and always with the same purpose of helping her race go forward. She established a school for delinquent girls in Ocala, Florida; opened several mission schools for children in turpentine camps; and helped to secure a hospital for Daytona. There is hardly an influential organization devoted to the welfare of Negroes in which she has not played an important role. In 1935 she was awarded the Spingarn medal for the outstanding achievement of her race during the previous year. She is director of the work among Negroes of the National Youth Administration. She has held the offices of President of Florida State Teachers' Association and Vice-President of the National Wage Earner's Association.

As a public speaker Mrs. Bethune has few superiors among women. Her effectiveness lies in her earnestness and in her natural eloquence. She has a tremendous appeal to young people, both white and colored. After lecturing at Vassar more than twoscore young women crowded into her room and plied her with questions on vocations for women, rights of women, and race relations. She answered all their questions frankly and honestly.

Mrs. Bethune has known poverty and disappointments which would have discouraged a less courageous person. Like other members of her race, she has found many doors closed to her in America, but her success is all the more remarkable when considered in the light of this fact. She has met obstacles and faced many difficulties, but always with a conquering spirit. She is indeed a worthy pioneer of an advancing race.

"LOVE YOUR NEIGHBOR" (to be told in story form): [79]

There was a youth of America who stood and said fervently,

— 160 —

"Thee, Lord, I love with all my heart and soul and mind and strength."

But He answered, "That is not enough. You are also to love your neighbor as yourself."

"Who is my neighbor, Lord?" she said.

And the Lord replied: "There are little children wearing out their lives in factories in every state in your nation. 'They are not my children,' you said, and pass by on the other side. There is a woman in your town who fell among unfriendly folk who stripped her of her reputation, and lashed her with their tongues, who froze her with their scorn, and left her half-dead in her soul. And all the 'respectable' women went by on the other side. There was a foreign woman who came to live in your town, homesick, baffled by strange customs in a strange land. And you, who were so busy with many things, looked at her, and went by on the other side. There was an intelligent girl trying to get an education in order that she might live life more abundantly, and you laughed at her efforts because her skin was different in color from yours. There was an industrial girl striking for a living wage for her family and her friends, and you yawned over the newspaper account of her efforts and deplored the inconvenience the strike caused you. There is a woman in your kitchen who is a human being; a man in your garden; a woman who lives in your street; a church seeking in its way to bring in the kingdom—but it is not your church! There are backward races of people groping for life and freedom; confused nations, great and small, trying dimly to find the way to give their gifts to the common life of the world. Human beings! Neighbors all!

"And you are to love your neighbor as much as yourself."

POEM: *"Awareness"* [80]

> God—let me be aware.
> Let me not stumble blindly down the ways,
> Just getting somehow safely through the days,
> Not even groping for another hand,
> Not even wondering why it all was planned,
> Eyes to the ground unseeking for the light,
> Soul never aching for a wild-winged flight,
> Please, keep me eager just to do my share.
> God—let me be aware.

God—let me be aware.
Stab my soul fiercely with others' pain,
Let me walk seeing horror and stain.
Let my hands, groping, find other hands.
Give me the heart that divines, understands.
Give me the courage, wounded, to fight.
Flood me with knowledge, drench me in light.
Please, keep me eager just to do my share.
God—let me be aware.

—MIRIAM TEICHNER.

PRAYER:

O Thou who art the Father of us all, we thank Thee that we are Thy children. Help us to overcome any prejudice, hatred, or lack of sympathy which would keep us from living in harmony with those about us. If we are harboring any ideas which make for exclusiveness, grant that we may rid ourselves of them. Help us to drive out all influences which keep us from being one in spirit and in truth. Give us a greater desire to co-operate in such a manner as will make for the common good of all. Disturb our complacency and satisfaction with ourselves and awaken us to the needs of those about us. Forgive us for our greed and selfishness which has caused us to keep for ourselves the things which we should share with others. Forgive us if we have disregarded the sacredness of personality. Forgive us for any act of ours which would tend to destroy Thy family, and hasten the day when we shall live together as brothers and sisters of a common Father. Through Jesus our Lord, we pray. AMEN.

HYMN: *"O Jesus, Prince of Life and Truth."*

BENEDICTION:

Send us forth, Our Father, in the power of Thy strength, that we may live together as sons and daughters of Thine. AMEN.

GROUP VI

Special Occasions

CANDLE LIGHTING

SERVICE XXVI. LIGHTED LAMPS

AIM: To lead to a desire to pledge one's self to a faithful discharge of responsibility both as officer and member of the group.

INSTRUMENTAL PRELUDE: Hymn tune, *"Creation"* (HAYDN).

CALL TO WORSHIP:

Leader:

> O Splendor of God's glory bright,
> O Thou that bringest light from light . . .
> Let fall in royal radiance
> Thy spirit's sanctifying beam,
> Upon our earthly senses stream.
> —AMBROSE OF MILAN.

Response (to be sung):

> Holy, holy, holy, Lord God of Hosts,
> Heaven and earth are full of Thy glory:
> Glory be to Thee, O Lord Most High. AMEN.

RESPONSIVE READING:

Leader: And God said, Let there be light: and there was light . . . the greater light to rule the day, and the lesser light to rule the night.

Response (to be sung):

> O worship the King, all glorious above,
> O gratefully sing His power and His love;

Our Shield and Defender, the Ancient of Days,
Pavilioned in splendor, and girded with praise.

Leader: And God said, Let there be a firmament in the midst of the
waters, and let it divide the waters from the waters.

Response:

O tell of His might, O sing of His grace,
Whose robe is the light, whose canopy space;
Whose chariots of wrath the deep thunderclouds form,
And dark is His path on the wings of the storm.

Leader: And God said, Let the waters under the heavens be gathered
together unto one place, and let the dry land appear. and it was so.

Response:

The earth with its store of wonders untold,
Almighty, Thy power hath founded of old;
Hath stablished it fast by a changeless decree,
And round it hath cast, like a mantle, the sea.

Leader: And God said, Let the earth put forth grass, herbs yielding
seed, and fruit-trees bearing fruit. . . . Let the waters swarm with
living creatures, and let birds fly above the earth.

Response:

Thy bountiful care what tongue can recite?
It breathes in the air, it shines in the light;
It streams from the hills, it descends to the plain,
And sweetly distils in the dew and the rain.

Leader: And God said, Let us make man in our image, after our likeness. . . . And God created man in his own image, in the image
of God created he him.[81]

Response:

Frail children of dust, and feeble as frail,
In Thee do we trust, nor find Thee to fail;
Thy mercies how tender, how firm to the end,
Our Maker, Defender, Redeemer, and Friend.

DOXOLOGY:

Praise God, from whom all blessings flow;
Praise Him, all creatures here below;
Praise Him above, ye heavenly host;
Praise Father, Son, and Holy Ghost.

SPECIAL MUSIC: *"Let There Be Light, Lord God of Hosts"* (quartet).

STORY:

"THE CHURCH OF LIGHTED LAMPS" [82]

LATE in the afternoon a stranger arrived in a tiny European village hidden among the mountains, far away from the beaten track of tourists. After looking around the quaint rooms she had engaged at the inn, she started out on an inspection tour of the village. She wandered about the narrow, winding streets, until, rounding a curve, she saw stretching before her a beautiful mountain path. Following it, she came to a little chapel which, with its ivy-covered walls and open door, invited her to enter.

She stepped inside and settled down for a quiet moment of meditation in one of the rustic pews. A strange feeling of peace pervaded the place. As she bowed her head in prayer, she thought of the many generations of simple peasant folk who had worshiped there, and felt strangely linked with them in fellowship. When she arose to go she noticed at the back of each pew a strange sort of framework; she also noticed the lack of lamps or lights of any sort in the place.

She returned to the inn and her pleasant room overlooking the village street. The sun set in splendor over the mountains and the shades of evening began to gather. The people of the village, having completed their day's work, gathered in the square, where the sound of merry laughter was heard. Then, as the twilight began to deepen, the people, singly and in pairs, began to make their way toward the little chapel. At last the mystery of the afternoon was solved, for each person was carrying a lantern.

The stranger, eager to learn more of the customs of the village, hastily followed, moving along the street which led uphill to the little church. As she entered, only the outline of the pews and pulpit could be seen by the dim flicker of light. But the worshipers continued to come. As each person entered and placed his lighted lamp in the rack provided for it at the back of the pew, he bowed his head in reverent prayer. The stranger bowed her head also.

When she raised her head after some moments of meditation and prayer, the lights were stronger and brighter. Now she could see the figure of the Christ carved above the altar, and other figures carved on the simple Communion table. By this time the church was almost filled with worshipers. As the people continued to gather, the light became still brighter, bringing into clearer detail every feature of the chapel, until finally the words inscribed over the archway were revealed: "Ye are the light of the world."

Finally the pastor mounted the pulpit and, by the light cast by the lanterns of the worshipers, read the Scripture for the evening and prayed this prayer: "O Thou who art the light of all lights, shed Thy radiance upon us. Grant that we may reflect Thy light and love in the world. May we let our light so shine before men that we may glorify Thee. For the sake of Him who came to be the Light of the world, we pray. Amen."

When the stranger inquired further concerning their strange custom, a legend was told her about "The Church of Lighted Lamps." It was built long ago in the sixteenth century by an old duke who had ten beautiful daughters whom he loved devotedly. When they were children he took great pleasure in watching them play, and even when they were grown he would sit in the garden for hours listening to their singing over their needlework, or watching them as they picked armfuls of roses.

Unlike most royal fathers, he was not anxious for them to marry, and it was with great reluctance that he let them go one by one. People used to smile at the commotion he made over each one leaving home, but he would shake his head sadly and say that each one had her place and that the house was lonely in some spot without her.

Each year the daughters gathered around their father's board to partake of the Christmas feast together. The circle had never been broken at this time until one year a daughter who had married a prince in a far country thought the journey too far, and decided not to go home. Knowing how much her father counted on this family gathering, she sent a band of musicians from her court to play for him, thinking to lighten his disappointment. But the duke was inconsolable. The songs of the musicians sounded artificial in comparison with his daughter's singing, for nothing could take her place.

As he grew older the duke began to wonder what he would leave behind to perpetuate his memory. Finally he decided to build a church so beautiful that men would worship as soon as they entered because it would draw them to God. He drew the plans and watched the building with great delight.

At last came the great day when all was finished and the duke took one of his daughters to see it. The simple lines, the graceful beams, the carving, and the stained glass windows were exclaimed over and admired.

"But, father," said the daughter, "where are the lamps to hang?"

"That, my dear," said the duke, "is a pet scheme of mine. There will be no hanging lamps. Each one will carry his own. I have provided small bronze lamps, one for every person in the village up to the number the church will hold." Then, he added slowly, "Some corner of God's house will be dark and lonely, if all his sons and daughters do not come to worship Him at the appointed time." And these words were carved in the stone over the doorway.

Four hundred years have elapsed since that time. The bronze lamps have been handed down from father to son and carefully treasured. When the sweet-toned bells of the old church ring, the village people wend their way up the hill, each carrying his own lamp. The church is nearly always filled, for no family wishes its corner to be dark and gloomy.

HYMN: *"Lord, Speak to Me, That I May Speak."*

INSTALLATION OF OFFICERS: [83]

Leader (to newly elected president):

You have been chosen by your group to lead them in the task of building the Kingdom of God. In this place of leadership to which you have been chosen, it will be your privilege to inspire your co-laborers with a zeal and enthusiasm for the task ahead. You will strive to direct all those who labor with you in such a manner as to bring about a spirit of co-operation and a high type of efficiency. You will endeavor to lead them into ever-widening fields of service and into nobler achievements.

To all other newly elected officers:

As you accept this place of leadership to which you have been selected, it becomes your privilege to lead your fellow workers into experiences which will enrich their own lives and forward the Master's cause. Are you willing to "study to show yourselves approved unto God, workmen that need not be ashamed"? Are you willing to accept the privileges and responsibilities which are yours because of the offices to which you have been elected? Do you pledge yourselves to a faithful discharge of the duties which you have assumed?

Response (by the newly elected officers): We dedicate ourselves to the faithful performance of our duties.

CANDLE-LIGHTING SERVICE: [84]

President: As I light this candle it brings to my mind the life of Jesus. May the love of Jesus so enter our lives that it will send us forth with a sincere desire to serve him.

Response: Thy word, O God, is a lamp unto my feet and a light unto my path. Incline our hearts to keep thy commandments.

First Officer: Behold, I kindle the light of humility. A Christian is humble and unselfish.

Response: Blessed are the poor in spirit: for theirs is the kingdom of heaven.

Second Officer: Behold, I kindle the light of meekness. A Christian is gentle and teachable, desiring nothing for himself, except an opportunity to serve.

Response: Blessed are the meek; for they shall inherit the earth.

Third Officer: Behold, I kindle the light which represents the growth of the Christian life. A Christian has a positive hunger for righteousness.

Response: Blessed are they which do hunger and thirst after righteousness: for they shall be filled.

Fourth Officer: Behold, I kindle the light of mercy. A Christian is considerate toward the failure and shortcomings of others.

Response: Blessed are the merciful: for they shall obtain mercy.

Fifth Officer: Behold, I kindle the light of purity. A Christian gives supreme loyalty to the right.

Response: Blessed are the pure in heart: for they shall see God.

Sixth Officer: Behold, I kindle the light of peace. A Christian is peace-loving at all times.

Response: Blessed are the peacemakers: for they shall be called the children of God.

President: A Christian endures suffering, criticism, and persecution courageously for Christ's sake. As we commit ourselves to the cause of Christ, may His spirit of self-sacrifice be central in our lives. Grant that the fires which have been lighted in our hearts this evening burn brightly evermore. I therefore beseech you to walk worthily of the calling wherewith ye were called, with all lowliness and meekness, with long-suffering, forbearing one another in love.

Response: We dedicate our time and our talents to this work to which we have been called.

HYMN: *"O Jesus, I Have Promised."*

BENEDICTION:

> Father, accept the worship we bring,
> To every one Thy strength impart,
> And shed Thy spirit in every heart.

GROUP VI

Special Occasions

CAMP

SERVICE XXVII. LETTING GO OF LESSER VALUES

(A GALILEAN SERVICE)

AIM: To lift up for the consideration of the group the proper relation of lesser values as compared to higher values, and to lead to a choice of higher values.

SOLO: Hymn tune of Ar Hyd Y Nos (*Trumpet*—played at a distance).

HYMN: *"Jesus Calls Us O'er the Tumult"* (sung by the group in the boats as they approach the shore).

SCRIPTURE READING:

The earth is the Lord's, and the fullness thereof;
The world, and they that dwell therein.
For He hath founded it upon the seas,
And established it upon the floods.
Who shall ascend into the hill of the Lord?
Or who shall stand in His holy place?
He that hath clean hands, and a pure heart;
Who hath not lifted up his soul unto vanity, nor sworn deceitfully.
He shall receive the blessing from the Lord,
And righteousness from the God of his salvation.[85]

HYMN: *"Now on Land and Sea Descending"* (to be sung antiphonally).

Now, on land and sea descending,
  Brings the night its peace profound;
Let our vesper hymn be blending
  With the holy calm around.
    (To be sung by chorus in boats)

Jubilate (sung by chorus in boats)!
Jubilate (response by group on shore!)
Jubilate (by chorus in boats)!
Amen (response by group on shore)!
Let our vesper hymn be blending
  With the holy calm around. (In unison.)

Soon as dies the sunset glory,
  Stars of heaven shine out above,
Telling still the ancient story—
  Their Creator's changeless love.
    (To be sung by chorus in boats.)

Jubilate! Jubilate! Jubilate! Amen!
Telling still the ancient story—
  Their Creator's changeless love.

STORY:

"THE PEARL OF GREAT PRICE" [86]

ONE SUMMER's morning a stranger, gorgeously arrayed, appeared in
the streets of the fishing village. Over a crimson silk tunic he wore a
gaily embroidered cloak, his white linen headpiece shone with gold
and silver threads, and from his belt hung a huge pouch embroidered
with every color of the rainbow. The children fairly tumbled out of
their houses to gaze at him.

"What can this splendid stranger wish here?" they whispered to
one another, and after he had stopped to ask a lad where he could
find the fishermen, the whole villageful of children followed the de-
lighted boy as he led the visitor down the narrow path to the beach.

There they found many of their fathers cleaning and mending
fish nets, or repairing the boats turned keel upward upon the sand.
They rose at the approach of the stranger and listened with interest
to his request. He was a merchant, he said, and had come this way
in search of pearls. Then, opening his rainbow pouch, he drew out

— 171 —

a handful of such perfect pearls that the children, as well as the fathers, exclaimed with wonder.

"See," said the merchant, holding up one large gem for all to gaze upon, "you who spend days and nights in the open see many colors in the changing sky, and will understand why I call this gem, full of rosy color, my pearl of the sunrise."

He replaced it and brought out another.

"Your work carries you at all hours," he said, "upon the waves; and you watch them change from blue to green, crested with creamy foam. This, then, is my pearl of the sea." Through the soft misty surface shone such perfect reflections of the waves' colors that one little child clapped her hands with delight.

"Yonder, against the turquoise sky," continued the merchant, "there stands a mountain crowned with gleaming snow. Does this, my pearl of the snowdrift, not seem like a bit of the mountain top itself?" He held up a third pearl, its white frosty surface gleaming like moonlight upon newly fallen snow.

"Many more goodly pearls do I possess," said the stranger, "and yet I am never content. I am seeking a stone containing all these colors combined, a pearl which will glisten like the snow, turn rosy as sunrise clouds, and gleam like the waves breaking under a blue sky. I know that such a gem would be of great price, but I am willing to sell all I possess to purchase it. Has any man among you seen or heard of such a one?"

"There is a fisherman at the other end of the lake," said one of the men, "who has found many wonderful pearls. He used to sell them to the lady Mary of Magdala, but she has left this part of the country; 'tis said she has become a follower of the Christ and her jewels are scattered among the poor and needy. Possibly if you journey to the home of the old fisherman you may find what you seek."

The merchant thanked the men and smiled gravely at the children. Although his gorgeous raiment and wonderful pearls fascinated them, they gazed at the man himself with awe; he looked so proud and stately with his deep-set dark eyes and flowing beard. They watched him, however, until he was out of sight, his robes gleaming like a hummingbird's breast, and wondered if they would ever see him again, or hear whether he found the perfect pearl for which he sought.

Days passed, and then one evening a fisherman, who had sailed with his little daughter across the lake to sell fish, came back with a strange and thrilling tale.

"I have seen the Christ," he cried, as his friends gathered around him. "He stood upon the mountainside, surrounded by crowds who had traveled from all directions in search of him. When I joined them he was not talking about anything curious or hard to understand; he was speaking of things we see and work with every day, a fish net, a harvest, and the making of bread. He told us that the kingdom of heaven was like these things, very precious and yet simple and open to all. He said that it was also like a merchantman seeking goodly pearls; who, when he had found one pearl of great price, went and sold all that he had and bought it.

"When he said these words I heard an exclamation of surprise behind me and, turning, I beheld the merchant who was here a short time ago. His eyes, as he gazed at Jesus, were burning with excitement. 'Ah, Thou thyself shineth among men as this pearl of great price shineth among other gems!' he cried. Then I saw that he was holding in his hand a pearl so glorious that if the eyes of the crowd had not been fastened upon the Master's face they would have looked with wonder at the gem. It was large and perfectly round, and its colors were beautiful beyond description. Think of a rainbow glowing across the sky, and you can best imagine the hues which melted one into the other in that wonderful jewel.

"Glancing at his pouch, I saw that it hung limp and empty at his side, and I knew that he must have sold all he possessed to buy this pearl of great price."

"'The Kingdom of Heaven,' repeated the merchant to himself; 'surely this gracious and kindly man is speaking of a realm over which he will rule. I will ask him to let me join him; for I, who have spent my life among all that is rich and rare, will certainly be given a high position in such a kingdom.'"

"Possibly some of the disciples overheard the merchant's words, for I heard one of them say to the Master, 'Who is greatest in the Kingdom of Heaven?' and the merchant behind me leaned forward eagerly to listen."

"And then," said the fisherman, "what happened next seems too wonderful to be true. For the Lord turned toward the spot where I was standing with my little girl, Hannah, and stretching out his hand called the child to him. She is so shy and timid that, as you know, she flees from strangers, but at the Master's words she left my side and ran to him as swiftly as a bird answers the call of its mate.

"Jesus took her in his arms and she nestled back as if she belonged there, while the crowd looked on, silent and perplexed. Then the voice of the Master rang out again.

" 'Verily I say unto you,' he said, 'Except ye become as little children, ye shall not enter into the Kingdom of Heaven. Whosoever therefore shall humble himself as this little child, the same is greatest in the Kingdom of Heaven, and whosoever shall receive one such little child in my name receiveth me; for he that is least among you, the same shall be great.'

"Again I heard the merchant give a sharp exclamation; but whether it was of disappointment or merely astonishment I could not tell.

" 'My pearl,' he murmured to himself, 'my pearl of great price,' and clasping the wonderful jewel tightly in his hand, he turned and made his way through the crowd away from Jesus."

Months passed, and a season of want came to the fishing village. For the fishing was poor, the crops failed, and there was much of hunger and illness among the children.

Jesus had traveled across the mountains; and although the people often spoke of him and longed for a sight of his face to comfort them, he did not return to that part of the country.

And then, in his place perhaps, came the pearl merchant. He arrived at the village one evening at dusk, and his embroidered robe shone through the grayness like the wings of a gorgeous butterfly. He did not wait for the pale-faced children to come to their doors to greet him. As though he guessed what need there was in that sun-parched spot, he passed quietly in and out of the homes, bearing not pearls in his rainbow pouch, but white bread and soothing remedies and gold pieces, one of which he left in the hand of each boy and girl. Upon his face there was a smile as sweet and tender as the smile of a happy child.

"Some day," he said to little Hannah's father, into whose home he went last of all, "I hope to see the Master again. But already I have joined his kingdom, the kingdom of all who serve, for in ministering to little children I know that I am doing the work of my Lord."

"The perfect pearl has been sold," he added, "because I have found something more precious and more beautiful. At last, indeed, little

Hannah, my quest has ended, for I have learned that the Master, that Peerless One, is himself the Pearl of Great Price."

PRAYER:

> Dear Lord, who sought at dawn of day the solitary woods
> to pray,
> In quietness we come to seek Thy guidance for the coming
> day.
> O Master, who with kindly face at noon walked in the market
> place,
> We crave a brother's smile and song, when mingling in the
> human throng.
> Strong Pilot, who at midnight hour could calm the sea with
> gentle power,
> Grant us the skill to aid the bark of those who drift in storm
> and dark.
> As Thou at weary eventide communed upon the mountain-
> side,
> In reverent stillness now we ask Thy presence in the daily
> task.
>
> —W. L. CURRY.

BENEDICTION: *"Taps"*

> Day is done,
> Gone the sun
> From the lake,
> From the hills,
> From the sky.
> All is well,
> Safely rest,
> God is nigh.

HYMN: *"Jesus, Saviour, Pilot Me."* (Sung by group in boats as they row out of sight. Those on shore remain seated and in silent meditation until last sound of music dies.)

SERVICE XXVIII: THE VISION SPLENDID

AIM: To lead to a clearer conception of God through a greater appreciation of the universe which He has created.

INSTRUMENTAL PRELUDE: *"On Wings of Song"* (MENDELSSOHN).

CALL TO WORSHIP:

> All nature's work His praise declare,
> To whom they all belong;
> There is a voice in every star,
> In every breeze a song.
> Sweet music fills the world abroad
> With strains of love and power;
> The stormy sea sings praise to God,
> The thunder and the shower.
>
> To God the tribes of ocean cry,
> And birds upon the wing;
> To God the powers that dwell on high
> Their tuneful tribute bring.
> Like them, let man the throne surround,
> With them loud chorus raise,
> While instruments of loftier sound
> Assist his feeble praise.
>
> —REV. HENRY WARE, JR.

LITANY OF ADORATION:

Leader: God that made the world and all things therein, he, being

Lord of heaven and earth, dwelleth not in temples made with hands;

Response: God's name be praised.

Leader: Neither is he served by men's hands, as though he needed anything, seeing he himself giveth to all life, and breath, and all things.

Response: God's name be praised.

Leader: He is not far from each one of us; for in him we live, and move, and have our being.

Response: God's name be praised.

Leader: O Lord, my God, thou art very great; thou art clothed with honor and majesty: who coverest thyself with light as with a garment:

Response: God's name be praised.

Leader: Who laid the foundations of the earth. Thou coveredst it with the deep as with a garment: the waters stood above the mountains. Thou hast set a bound that they may not pass over; that they turn not again to cover the earth.

Response: God's name be praised.

Leader: He appointed the moon for seasons: the sun knoweth his going down.

Response: God's name be praised.

Leader: O Lord, how manifold are thy works! in wisdom hast thou made them all: the earth is full of thy riches.[87]

Response: God's name be praised, forever and forever.

DOXOLOGY: Praise God, from whom all blessings flow;
Praise Him, all creatures here below;
Praise Him above, ye heavenly host:
Praise Father, Son, and Holy Ghost. AMEN.

PRAYER: *"For This World."* [88]

O God, we thank Thee for this universe, our great home; for its vastness and its riches, and for the manifoldness of the life which teems upon it and of which we are a part. We praise Thee for the arching sky and the blessed winds, for the driving clouds and the constellations on high. We praise Thee for the salt sea and the running water, for the everlasting hills, for the trees, and for the grass under our feet. We thank Thee for our senses by which we can see the splendor of the morning, and hear the jubilant songs of love, and

—177—

smell the breath of the springtime. Grant us, we pray Thee, a heart wide open to all this joy and beauty, and save our souls from being so steeped in care or so darkened by passion that we pass heedless and unseeing when even the thornbush by the wayside is aflame with the glory of God. AMEN.

HYMN: *"God of the Earth, the Sky, the Sea"*

> God of the earth, the sky, the sea!
>   Maker of all above, below!
> Creation lives and moves in Thee,
>   Thy present life through all doth flow.
>
> Thy love is in the sunshine's glow,
>   Thy life is in the quickening air;
> When lightnings flash and storm-winds blow,
>   There is Thy power; Thy law is there.
>
> We feel Thy calm at evening's hour,
>   Thy grandeur in the march of night;
> And, when Thy morning breaks in power,
>   We hear Thy word, "Let there be light."
>
> We give Thee thanks, Thy name we sing,
> Almighty Father, heavenly King.
>   —SAMUEL LONGFELLOW.

POEM: *"The Gray Hills Taught Me Patience"* [89]

> The gray hills taught me patience,
>   The waters taught me prayer;
> The flight of birds unfolded
>   The marvel of thy care.
>
> The calm skies made me quiet,
>   The high stars made me still;
> The bolts of thunder taught me
>   The lightning of Thy will.
>
> Thy soul is on the tempest,
>   Thy courage rides the air.
> Through heaven or hell I'll follow;
>   I must—and so I dare !
>   —ALLEN EASTMAN CROSS.

Hymn: *"In Life's Earnest Morning,"* or
"I Would Be True."

Story:

"THE LEGEND OF WOWASSA" [90]

Out on the western plains before the white man came there lived with his peace-loving tribe an Indian lad named Wowassa. Dwelling in the shadows of the great mountains, these Indians had learned the secrets of great power. Other tribes had seen their dwelling place, but had left it to seek better hunting grounds. Yet, for the people of Wowassa's tribe, this flat, rolling country, bounded on the west by great peaks, held a secret charm.

From his mother Wowassa learned of firewood, tepees, earthern pots, and all the homely arts of living. When his legs had grown steady and his eyes keen enough to catch the slightest movement on the plains, his father taught him how to find the straightest branches, how to chip the flint for arrowheads, how to bind the feathers to the shaft, and how to hunt for game. And as he learned the games and sports of youth, he felt the tingle of new strength in his veins.

Young manhood came and with it at last the summons to the High Council. Cross-legged before the council fire sat the aged Chieftain. Wowassa listened as his venerable leader recounted the story of the tribe. At the conclusion he said: "To the westward far across the foothills is 'The Mountain of the Chieftain.'"

Though he gave no sign, Wowassa remembered how often in his childhood he had turned his face toward this the highest of all peaks and wondered why it was called "The Mountain of the Chieftain." Perhaps it would be explained to him now.

The aged Chieftain continued: "According to the ancient custom of our people, he who would be chief among us must some day climb to yonder summit. Many have been the seasons since I have looked upon its lofty peaks. Age is now coming fast upon me, and one of you must be the chief."

In the silence of the Council Wowassa's muscles strained and his heart beat faster. Dared he give himself in trial? Dared he brave the mountain's dangers? Quick as a flash the decision was made. With a look of determination and with a firm step he and two other brave lads strode across the open space and stood before the Chieftain.

The words of the aged leader were brief: "Only one thing I ask:

Bring me, in your hands, a token of your journey's end. Now, go!"

There followed days of anxious wonder and nights of weary waiting. Out across the westward plains had gone the tribe's three strongest braves. About the council circle each evening the warriors gathered. In the next circle were the braves and far out in the flickering shadows crouched the squaws with their papooses. In silence they waited.

Then there came a night of tense expectancy. From the westward there could be seen two moving forms. Every member of the tribe gathered about the council circle. Hours passed as they eagerly waited. Then out of the darkness came the footfalls of returning braves. Into the circle of light came Nakado, fleet of foot, and stood before the chief. In his extended hand there lay a tiny leaf, exquisitely shaped and beautifully colored.

"O Great Chief," spoke Nakado, "in the bleakness of the mountainside, from the hardness of winter forest, I have learned to see the wonders of Wokanda. Is it not beautiful?"

"Beauty is in deeds well done, my son," said the chief. "Beauty lies only at the journey's end—you had barely reached the lowest mountain. Not for you is the council's honor."

And Nakado bowed his head with heaviness of heart.

Then into the circle of faces came Mowona, "He That Seeketh." Proudly he bore to the council bronzed hands filled with golden nuggets.

"Far upon the mountainside, in the face of dangerous hardships, did I seek this hidden wealth, O Chief," said he, as he extended his hands filled with nuggets.

"Wealth lies beyond the touch of hands. Why did you stop there?" inquired the chief.

And Mowona turned away sorrowfully.

Then came anxious days and councils of grave import. The strongest and bravest of the tribe was still out there in the cold and danger. He was yonder among hungry wolves and stealthy panthers. Was his strength sufficient for all the dangers that he must face? On the plains the council waited.

There were moments when the wind in the pine trees did not even whisper. At last into the council came Wowassa, footsore and weary. With slow steps he circled the council and stood at last before the chief. Every heart beat faster and steady eyes scanned his bronzed and hardened figure.

Then steadily Wowassa moved his clenched hands before him. Every warrior's muscles strained as though to help him lift a heavy weight. Then suddenly Wowassa opened his hands. Eyes burst wide in disappointed wonder—for his hands were empty.

Then spoke Wowassa: "O Great Chief, where I stood there was nothing to bring. But, O Chief, where I stood I could see the Vision Splendid—the shining sea!"

The young warrior took his seat in the council as the chief of the tribe, and the people knew that the selection was wise, because Wowassa had obtained the vision splendid.

PRAYER:

Create within our hearts a desire for the vision splendid. Give us a vision of the person we may become through Thy power and strength. May we put aside trivial things that would retard us. Grant that we may strive to make our visions become actual realities in our lives, that Thou mayest see reflected in us the beauty and truth of Jesus. AMEN.

HYMN: *"Christ of the Upward Way,"* or
      "To the Knights in the Days of Old,"
      "O Thou Whose Feet Have Climbed Life's Hill."

BENEDICTION:

O Thou who dost the vision send, grant unto us strength sufficient to live according to Thy truth as it has been revealed to us. AMEN.

EASTER

SERVICE XXIX: TRANSFORMATION

AIM: To lead to an awareness of the transformation which may be wrought in one's life by striving to live the victorious life that Jesus lived.

INSTRUMENTAL PRELUDE: *"Morning Mood,"* from Peer Gynt Suite (EDVARD GRIEG).

CALL TO WORSHIP:

Leader: Jesus Christ is risen today,
Our triumphant holy day.

Response: Hymns of praise then let us sing
Unto Christ, our heavenly King.

Leader: Sing we to our God above,
Praise eternal as His love;

Response: Praise Him, all ye heavenly host,
Father, Son, and Holy Ghost.
—CHARLES WESLEY.

HYMN: *"Joyful, Joyful, We Adore Thee,"* or
"O Joyous Easter Morning."

LITANY OF PRAISE:

Leader: Praise ye the Lord. Praise ye the Lord from the heavens: praise him in the heights.

Response: Praise his holy name.

Leader: Praise ye him, all his angels: praise ye him, all ye stars of light.

Response: Praise his holy name.

Leader: Kings of earth, and all people; princes, and all judges of the earth.

Response: Let all the people praise him.

Leader: Let them praise the name of the Lord: for his name alone is excellent; his glory is above the earth and heaven.

Response: Praise ye the Lord.[91]

SCRIPTURE:

The first day of the week cometh Mary Magdalene early, when it was yet dark, unto the sepulcher, and seeth the stone taken away from the sepulcher. Then she runneth, and cometh to Simon Peter, and to the other disciple, whom Jesus loved, and saith unto them, They have taken away the Lord out of the sepulcher, and we know not where they have laid him. . . .

But Mary stood without at the sepulcher weeping: and as she wept, she stooped down, and looked into the sepulcher, and seeth two angels in white sitting, the one at the head, and the other at the feet, where the body of Jesus had lain. And they say unto her, Woman, why weepest thou? She saith unto them, Because they have taken away my Lord, and I know not where they have laid him. And when she had thus said, she turned herself back, and saw Jesus standing, and knew not that it was Jesus. Jesus saith unto her, Woman, why weepest thou? whom seekest thou? She, supposing him to be the gardener, saith unto him, Sir, if thou have borne him hence, tell me where thou hast laid him, and I will take him away. Jesus saith unto her, Mary. She turned herself, and saith unto him, Rabboni; which is to say, Master. Jesus saith unto her, Touch me not; for I am not yet ascended to my Father: but go to my brethren, and say unto them, I ascend unto my Father, and your Father; and to my God, and your God. Mary Magdalene came and told the disciples that she had seen the Lord, and that he had spoken these things unto her.[92]

SPECIAL MUSIC: *"O Beautiful Eastertide"* [93]

O beautiful the Eastertide
That broke the bars of night,

And flung the sable portals wide,
  And flooded earth with light;
O Eastertide, glad Eastertide,
  That rolled the stone away,
And hailed the Christ men sacrificed,
  King of Eternal day.

O beautiful the Eastertide
  That on God's children shone
When grief and fear together tried
  To hurl hope from the throne;
O Eastertide, sweet Eastertide,
  That wiped away their tears,
And gave them power for that dread hour,
  And banished all their fears!

O beautiful the Eastertide
  That makes the lilies bloom,
And sounds the joy-note far and wide,
  And glorifies the tomb;
O Eastertide, fair Eastertide,
  That sets our faith aflame,
And leads us on where Christ has gone
  In His eternal name!
                    —Chauncey R. Piety.

"Affirmation of Faith" (in unison):

I believe that the life everlasting flows from the Fatherhood of God as the stream from the spring.

I believe that the Risen Christ is the visible witness to the sublime truth that the grave has no victory, and death no sting.

I believe that immortality is something to be lived rather than something to be proved.

I believe that the universe is God's house, that this world is not the only habitat of the living, but that in his house are many rooms.

I believe in holding daily life under the quiet light of eternity, and in pasturing our thoughts in the amazing love of God.[94]

STORY:

"THE BEAUTY OF THE LILY" [95]

ONCE UPON a time in a far-distant land there lived a peasant named Ivan [96] and his little nephew, Vassily. [97] Ivan was gloomy and unkempt, and his restless eyes looked out from matted hair which hung almost to his neglected beard. Little Vassily thought his uncle was kind enough to him, though he never washed him, nor combed his hair, nor taught him to do anything. The hut in which they lived was very miserable. Its walls were full of holes; the furniture of its one room was broken and dusty, and the floor was unswept. The garden was filled with stones and weeds. The neighbors only passed in the daytime, for fear of Ivan, and they always turned their heads.

It happened one Easter morning that Ivan, feeling restless, rose early and went and stood before the door of the hut. The trees were budding; the air was full of the songs of birds; the dew lay glittering on the grass, and a nearby brook ran leaping and gurgling along. The rays of the slanting sun shone on the tops of the distant hills, and seemed to touch the hut. As Ivan looked he saw a young man coming swiftly and lightly from the hills, and he bore on his arm a sheaf of pure, white lilies. The stranger drew near and stopped before the hut.

"Christ is risen!" he said in flutelike tones.

"He is risen, indeed!" muttered Ivan through his beard. Then the young man took a lily from his sheaf and gave it to Ivan, saying, "Keep it white!" and smiling, he passed on.

Wonderingly Ivan gazed at the flower in his hand. Its gold green stem seemed to support a pure white crown—or was it a translucent cup filled with light! And as the man looked into the flower's gold-fringed heart, awe stole into his soul. Then he turned and entered the hut, saying to himself, "I will put it in water."

But when he went to lay the lily on the window sill, that he might search for a vessel to put it in, he dared not put it down, for the sill was covered with thick dust. He turned to the table, but its top was soiled with crumbs of moldy bread and cheese, mingled with dirt. He looked about the room, but not one spot could he see where he might lay the lily without spoiling its loveliness. He searched for something in which to put it. He found an empty bottle which he carried to the brook and filled with the sparkling water. This he placed upon the table and in it set the lily.

Then he noticed the begrimed hands of little Vassily and thought, "When I leave the room, he might touch the flower and soil it." So he took the child, washed him, and combed his hair, and he seemed to bloom like the lily itself. Ivan looked upon him with amazement, murmuring, "I never saw it thus before."

From that hour a change came over Ivan. He washed himself and cleaned the hut. He sowed flowers and vegetables in the garden where the weeds had been. As for the lily, seven days it blossomed in freshness and beauty, and gave forth a delicate fragrance, but on the eighth day, when Ivan awoke, it withered. As Ivan and Vassily worked in the field from day to day, the neighbors stopped to talk with them. They told Ivan about the lilies of the field that toil not, neither do they spin, yet Solomon in all his glory was not arrayed like one of them.

So Easter came again, and very early Ivan and Vassily stood before the hut. When the splendor of the day rose above the distant hills, lo! the young man came swiftly and lightly. Stopping before the hut, he said: "Christ is risen!"

"He is risen, indeed!" responded Ivan and Vassily joyously.

"How beautiful is thy lily!" said the young man.

"Alas," said Ivan, "it is vanished."

"But its beauty lives in thy heart, therefore it can never die," said the young man, as he smiled tenderly at Ivan and passed on.

PRAYER:

O Thou living Christ, manifest Thyself to us. We thank Thee that Thou dost manifest Thyself to those who hunger and thirst after righteousness. We praise Thee that thou didst break the bonds of death on the first Easter, and appeared unto those whose hearts were prepared to receive Thee. Take away the dimness of our sight that we may see Thee more perfectly in all Thy mighty processes in the world today. Give unto us a vision of that higher life which we may enter if we are obedient unto Thy commands. Grant unto us the strength sufficient to live the victorious life. May Thy spirit dwell within us at all times, transforming us into the kind of followers that Thou wouldst have us be. In Thy name we pray. AMEN.

BENEDICTION.

GROUP VI

Special Occasions

ARMISTICE DAY

SERVICE XXX: NONRESISTANCE

Aim: To lead to a better understanding of the way in which peace may be brought to the world.

Instrumental Prelude: *"Largo"* (Handel).

Call to Worship:

> Down the dark future, through long generations,
>   The echoing sounds grow fainter and then cease;
> And like a bell, with solemn, sweet vibrations,
>   I hear once more the voice of Christ say, "Peace!"

> Peace! and no longer from its brazen portals
>   The blast of war's great organ shakes the skies!
> But beautiful as songs of the immortals,
>   The holy melodies of love arise.
>   —Henry W. Longfellow.

Responsive Reading:

Leader: God hath made of one blood all nations of men to dwell on all the face of the earth.[98]

Response (to be sung):

> Come! Peace of God, and dwell again on earth,
> Come, with the calm that hailed thy Prince's birth,
> Come, with the healing of thy gentle touch,
> Come, Peace of God, that this world needs so much.[99]

Leader: They shall beat their swords into plowshares, and their spears into pruning hooks: nation shall not lift up sword against nation, neither shall they learn war any more.[98]

Response:

> Break every weapon forged in fires of hate,
> Turn back the foes that would assail thy gate;
> Where fields of strife lie desolate and bare,
> Take thy sweet flowers of peace and plant them there.[99]

Leader: They shall come from the east, and from the west, and from the north, and from the south, and shall sit down in the kingdom of God.[98]

Response:

> Bring selfish lives from shadow-lands of loss
> Into the radiance of the Saviour's cross,
> Where, in that gift—so precious, yet so lone—
> Life finds its brotherhood and love its throne.[99]

Leader: For he is our peace, who hath made both one, and hath broken down the middle wall of partition between us.[98]

Response:

> Come! Blessed Peace, as when, in hush of eve,
> God's benediction falls on souls who grieve;
> As shines a star when weary day departs,
> Come, Peace of God, and rule within our hearts.[99]

—MARY ROWLAND.

PRAYER:

O Thou, who art the Father of all nations, and who desireth that all Thy children should live together as brothers, hear us as we pray for the peace of the world. Destroy the influences which create bitterness, hatred, and misunderstanding. Purge diplomacy and commerce of all that is unclean. Draw the nations of the world together with a stronger bond of brotherhood. Grant that we may have a spirit of co-operation which will lead us to work for the common good of all. May Thy peace come on earth, we pray in the name of the Prince of Peace. AMEN.

HYMN: *"A Hymn of Peace"* [100]

> The Son of God goes forth for Peace,
> Our Father's love to show;

From war and woe He brings release,
  O, who with him will go?
He strikes the fetters from the slave,
  Man's mind and heart makes free;
And sends his messengers to save
  O'er every land and sea!

The Son of God goes forth for peace,
  Nor lands nor power to gain;
He seeks to serve, to love, to lift;
  Who follows in His train?
A glorious band, in every age,
  In spite of scorn and pain,
True sons of God, his peace have made;
  Who follows in their train?

Now let the world to peace be won,
  And every hatred slain:
Let force and greed be overcome
  And love supreme remain!
Let justice rule in all the earth,
  And mercy while we live,
Lest we—forgiven much—forget
  Our brother to forgive!

We send our love to every land—
  True neighbors would we be;
And pray God's peace to reign in them,
  Where'er their homeland be!
O God, to us may grace be given,
  Who bear the dear Christ's name,
To live at peace with every man,
  And thus our Christ acclaim!
                    —ERNEST BOURNER ALLEN.

STORY:

"THE INVINCIBLE LEADER" [101]

TELL ME A STORY about when you were a great soldier. Tell me about one of the battles you won," said a little boy to his grandfather.

The old man had been a colonel in the Austrian army for many years and could recount fierce tales of conquest by his troops. But today he shook his head as he took the boy upon his knee.

"I will tell you, instead," he said, "of the greatest battle I ever lost, which was won by braver men than mine."

The little boy was astonished, for he thought that his grandfather's soldiers were the bravest in the world. So he listened eagerly.

"I was commanded," the old colonel began, "to march against a little town in the Tyrol and lay siege to it. We had been meeting stubborn resistance in that part of the country, but we felt sure that we should win because all the advantages were on our side. My confidence, however, was arrested by a remark from a prisoner we had taken. 'You will never take that town,' he said, 'for they have an Invincible Leader.'

"'What does the fellow mean?' I inquired of one of my staff. 'And who is this leader of whom he speaks?' Nobody seemed able to answer my question, and so, in case there should be some truth in the report, I doubled preparation.

"As we descended through the pass in the Alps, I saw with surprise that the cattle were still grazing in the valley and that women and children—yes, and even men—were working in the fields.

"'Either they are not expecting us, or this is a trap to catch us,' I thought to myself. As we drew nearer the town we passed people on the road. They smiled and greeted us with a friendly word, and then went on their way. So friendly was their attitude toward us, and so different from the usual reception given us, that my soldiers forgot they were under discipline and returned the greeting.

"Finally we reached the town and clattered up the cobble-paved streets—colors flying, horns sounding a challenge, arms in readiness. The forge of the blacksmith shop was glowing, and the smith left it to stand in the door with a number of others to watch us pass. Suddenly he waved to one of my soldiers and I heard him exclaim, 'I knew that fellow when we were boys together at Innsbruck.'

"Women came to the windows and doorways with little babies in their arms. Some of them looked startled and held the babies closer, then went quietly on with their household tasks without panic or confusion. As for the boys—little fellows like you, my son [the old man cuddled the boy in his arms], they made us feel as though we were taking part in a glorious parade for their special amusement. They swarmed after us, whooping with delight and asking innumerable questions about the weapons we carried. Apparently they had never seen guns and swords before.

"It was impossible to keep strict discipline, and I began to feel rather foolish. My soldiers answered the questions of the children, and I saw one old warrior throw a kiss to a little golden-haired tot on a doorstep. 'Just the size of my Liza,' he muttered.

"Still no sign of an ambush. We rode straight to the open square on which the town hall faced. Here, if anywhere, resistance was to be expected. This is what we found. The door of the beautiful old building was wide open. Pigeons flew up from the grass around the fountain as we approached. No cannon or barricade was in sight, and my regiment, as it poured into the square, looked out of place.

"Just as I had reached the hall and my guard was drawn up at attention, an old white-haired man, who by his insignia I surmised to be the mayor, stepped forth, followed by ten men in simple peasant costume. They were all dignified and unabashed by the armed force before them—the most terrible soldiers of the great army of Austria."

"And what did this old man say, in the face of your guns and your cannon?" asked the little boy breathlessly.

"He walked down the steps, straight to my horse's side, and with hand extended, cried, 'Welcome, brother!' One of my aides made a gesture as if to strike him down with his sword, but I saw by the face of the old mayor that this was no trick on his part.

" 'Where are your soldiers?' I demanded.

" 'Soldiers? Why, don't you know that we have none?' he replied.

" 'But we have come to take the town.'

" 'Well, no one will stop you.'

" 'Are there none here to fight?'

"At this question, the old man's face lit up with a rare smile that I will always remember. Often afterwards, when engaged in bloody warfare, I would suddenly see that man's smile—and somehow, I came to hate my business. His words were simply: 'No, there is no one here to fight. We have chosen Christ for our Leader, and he taught men another way.' "

"What did you do then, grandfather?" asked the little boy eagerly.

"Do you know, son," the old soldier answered, "there seemed

nothing left for us to do but to ride away, leaving the town unmolested. It was impossible to take it. If I had ordered my soldiers to fire on those smiling men, women, and children, I knew that they would not have obeyed me. Even military discipline has its limits. Could I command the grizzly soldier to shoot down the child that reminded him of his Liza? I reported to headquarters that the town had offered unassailable resistance, although this admission injured my military reputation. But I was right. We had literally been conquered by these simple folk who followed implicity the leadership of Jesus Christ."

POEM: *"O Prince of Peace"* [102]

O Prince of Peace, marshal thine own
  And battle War today;
His jealousies and hates dethrone,
  And tear his mask away,
And cast him out, oh, cast War out,
  Destroy his bloody sway.

O Prince of Peace, marshal thy host
  And battle War again;
Destroy his towers on every coast
  And still his voice and pen,
And cast him out, oh, cast War out
  From all the hearts of men.

O Prince of Peace, marshal thine own,
  Drive War from sea and shore,
And build in hearts of men thy throne,
  And holy love restore—
O Prince of Peace, O Prince of Peace,
  Come, reign forevermore.

      —CHAUNCEY R. PIETY.

LITANY OF SUPPLICATION:

Leader: Thou who art the author of peace, hear us as we pray for the peace of the world,

Response: O God, hear our prayer.

— 192 —

Leader: Grant that we may put out of our lives all hatred, prejudice, and selfishness, and make love the ruling motive of our lives,

Response: We humbly pray, O God.

Leader: Destroy all influences which bring about war,

Response: We beseech Thee, O God.

Leader: Come, Thou, and rule over us. Guide us in our national affairs,

Response: We beseech Thee, O God.

Leader: Give unto the President of the nation the wisdom to guide us in the way of peace.

Response: We beseech Thee, O God.

Leader: Bless Thy people everywhere, and hasten the day when righteousness shall cover the earth as the waters cover the sea.

Response: O God, hear our prayer for Jesus' sake. AMEN.

HYMN: *"God of the Nations, Near and Far,"* or
"God the Omnipotent,"
"Lift Up Our Hearts, O King of Kings."

BENEDICTION:

May the God of Peace rest and abide with you both now and forevermore. AMEN.

GROUP VI

Special Occasions

CHRISTMAS

SERVICE XXXI: O COME, LET US ADORE HIM

AIM: To understand more fully the meaning of Christmas and to bring worship which is appropriate to the season.

INSTRUMENTAL PRELUDE: *"Adoration"* (BOROWSKI), or music to the English Carol, "The First Noel."

CALL TO WORSHIP:

Come, Thou long-expected Jesus,
  Born to set Thy people free;
From our fears and sins release us;
  Let us find our rest in Thee.
Israel's Strength and Consolation,
  Hope of all the earth Thou art;
Dear Desire of every nation,
  Joy of every longing heart.

Born Thy people to deliver,
  Born a child and yet a King.
Born to reign in us forever,
  Now Thy gracious kingdom bring.
By Thine own eternal Spirit
  Rule in all our hearts alone;
By thine all-sufficient merit,
  Raise us to Thy glorious throne.

—CHARLES WESLEY.

— 194 —

HYMN: *"Joy to the World."*

STORY:

"THE FIRST CHRISTMAS ROSES" [103]

THE SUN had dropped below the western hills of Judea, and the stillness of night had covered the earth. The heavens were illumined only by numberless stars, which shone the brighter for the darkness of the sky. No sound was heard but the occasional howl of a jackal or the bleat of a lamb in the sheepfold. Inside a tent on the hillside slept the shepherd, Berachah, and his daughter, Madelon. The little girl lay restless—sleeping, waking, dreaming, until at last she roused herself and looked about her.

"Father, awake," she whispered, "I fear for the sheep."

The shepherd turned and reached for his staff. "What hearest thou, daughter? Hast thou been wakened by an evil dream?"

Berachah rose, looked over the hills toward Bethlehem, and listened. By the campfire below on the hillside the shepherds on watch were rousing themselves. Berachah waited and wondered. Suddenly a sound rang out in the stillness.

"It is the voice of an angel, my daughter. What it means I know not. Neither understand I this light."

As he fell on his knees he heard: "Fear not: for, behold, I bring you good tidings of great joy, which shall be to all people. For unto you is born this day in the city of David a Saviour, which is Christ the Lord. And this shall be a sign unto you: Ye shall find the babe wrapped in swaddling clothes, lying in a manger."

The voice of the angel died away, and the air was filled with music. Berachah raised Madelon to her feet. "Ah, daughter," said he, "it is the wonder night so long expected. To us hath it been given to see the sign. It is the Messiah who hath come, the Messiah whose name shall be Wonderful, Counsellor, the Mighty God, the Everlasting Father, the Prince of Peace. He it is who shall reign on the throne of David, he it is who shall redeem Israel."

Slowly up the hillside toiled the shepherds to the tent of Berachah, their chief, who rose to greet them eagerly.

"What think you of the wonder night and of the sign?" he queried. "Are we not above all others honored, thus to learn of the Messiah's coming?"

"Yes," replied their spokesman; "let us go to Bethlehem, and see this thing which has come to pass."

A murmur of protest came from the edge of the circle, and one or two whispered of duty toward the flocks. Hardheaded, practical men were these, whose hearts had not been touched by vision or by song.

The others, however, turned expectantly toward their chief, awaiting his decision. "Truly, the angel hath given us the sign in order that we might go to worship him. How can we then do otherwise? We shall find him, as we have heard, lying in a manger. Let us not tarry, but let us gather our choicest treasures to lay at his feet, and set out without delay across the hills toward Bethlehem."

"Oh, father, permit me to go with thee," begged Madelon. Berachah did not hear her, but turned and bade the men gather together their gifts.

Soon the shepherds returned with their gifts. Simple treasures they were, a pair of doves, a fine wool blanket, some honey, some late autumn fruits. Berachah had searched for the finest of his flock—a snow-white lamb. Across the hills toward Bethlehem in the quiet, starlit night they journeyed.

Following at a distance, yet close enough to see them, came Madelon with her dog. Over the hills they traveled until they lost sight of their own hillside. When at last they reached Bethlehem, they halted by an open doorway at a signal from their leader.

"The manger," they joyfully murmured, "the manger. We have found the new-born King!"

One by one they entered and fell on their knees. Away in the shadows stood the little girl, her hand on her dog's head. In wonder she gazed while the shepherds presented their gifts.

"Alas," she grieved, "no gift have I for the infant Saviour. Would that I had but a flower to place in his hand."

Suddenly the dog stirred and she saw one in white by her side. "Why grievest thou?" asked the one beside her.

"That I have no gift with which to greet him," she replied.

"The gift of thine heart, that is the best of all," came the reply.

And as Madelon looked she saw fair, white roses growing near by. Timidly she stretched out her hand and gathered them until her arms were filled. Again she turned toward the manger, and quietly slipped to the circle of kneeling shepherds. Closer she crept to the Child, longing, yet fearing to offer her gift.

"How shall I know," she pondered, "whether he will receive this gift?"

Berachah gazed in amazement at his daughter and the roses which she held. How came his child here, when he had left her safe on the hillside? Truly this was a wonder night.

Step by step she neared the manger, knelt and placed a rose in the baby's hand. As the shepherds watched in silence, Mary bent over the child, and Madelon waited for a sign.

"Will he accept them?" she questioned. "How shall I know?"

And as she prayed in humble silence, the Baby's eyes opened slowly and over his face spread a smile. And Madelon knew that her gift had been accepted.

RESPONSIVE READING:

Leader: The people that walked in darkness have seen a great light: they that dwell in the land of the shadow of death, upon them hath the light shined.

Response: For unto us a child is born, unto us a Son is given: and the government shall be upon his shoulders.

SOLO [104] (Traveler):

Watchman, Tell Us of the Night, What Its Signs of Promise Are.

SOLO (Watchman):

Traveler, O'er Yon Mountain's Height, See That Glory Beaming Star!

SOLO (Traveler):

Watchman, Doth Its Beauteous Ray Aught of Joy or Hope Foretell?

SOLO (Watchman):

Traveler, Yes; It Brings the Day, Promised Day of Israel.

Leader: And his name shall be called Wonderful, Counsellor, the Mighty God, the Everlasting Father, the Prince of Peace. Of the increase of his government and peace there shall be no end.

Response: Upon the throne of David, and upon his kingdom, to order it, and to establish it with judgment and with justice from henceforth even forever.

SOLO: (Divide the second and third stanzas of *Watchman, Tell Us of the Night,"* similar to the first stanza.)

TABLEAU: [105] *"The Prince of Peace."*

HYMN (sung by shepherds): [106] *"Silent Night, Holy Night."*

HYMN (sung by the Wise Men): [107] *"We Three Kings of the Orient Are."*

HYMNS (sung by group): *"O Little Town of Bethlehem," "O Come, All Ye Faithful."* [108]

PRAYER:

Our Father, we come to Thee with gratitude in our hearts for the gift of Thy Son to the world. We praise Thee for the joy which came to the world on that first Christmas, and which may be experienced anew each year. Grant that we may celebrate His birthday in a worshipful manner, and in our giving reflect His spirit. May we at this holiday season offer to Thee not only songs of praise, but may we offer our lives as well. Grant that Christ may be born again in our hearts, and may we follow His teachings more fully in the days that are ahead. Come, Thou Prince of Peace, and dwell with us forevermore. Send Thy blessings upon the world, our Father. May peace and good will come to all nations. Unite all people everywhere in the holy bonds of love. We bring this prayer in the name of Jesus whose birthday we celebrate. AMEN.

BENEDICTION:

The God of peace himself give you peace at all times, in all ways. The Lord be with you all. AMEN.

POSTLUDE: *"The Pastoral Symphony"* from *"The Messiah"* (HANDEL).

GROUP VII

Services for Intermediates

SERVICE XXXII: FEATHERS FOR WORMS

AIM: To lead to a desire to practice self-control and to obey the laws of health, thus building strong bodies.

INSTRUMENTAL PRELUDE: *"Andante Religioso"* (THOME).

CALL TO WORSHIP:

> Spirit of God, descend upon my heart;
> Wean it from earth; through all its pulses move;
> Stoop to my weakness, mighty as Thou art,
> And make me love Thee as I ought to love.
>
> Teach me to feel that Thou art always nigh;
> Teach me the struggles of the soul to bear,
> To check the rising doubt, the rebel sigh;
> Teach me the patience of unanswered prayer.
> —GEORGE CROLY.

HYMN: *"O Jesus, Once a Nazareth Boy."*

STORY:

"THE SKYLARK'S BARGAIN" [109]

THERE WAS once a young skylark who was very fond of worms. He used to say that he would give anything if he could make sure of getting all the worms he could eat.

One day as he was flying up into the sky, he looked down and saw something rather unusual traveling along the cart-track which ran through the forest. Feeling curious, the young skylark dropped lower and lower until at last he could see. O wonder—a queer sight indeed. He saw a tiny coach, painted black, with red blinds and yellow wheels, drawn by two magpies. Walking in front of the coach was an old man, very little and ugly, wearing a black coat with red trousers and yellow stockings. He carried a bell, and as he walked he kept swinging the bell and shouting:

> "Who will buy? Who will buy?
> I am selling in all weathers,
> Fine and fat and juicy worms,
> In exchange for skylark's feathers."

The skylark was attracted, and flew down. "Good morning, my young friend," said the old man. "What can I do for you?"

"How much are they?" asked the skylark.

"Two for a feather, my friend, and the coach is full of them."

"Are they fresh?" said the young bird.

"Yes, indeed; all gathered fresh this morning, my pretty bird."

The skylark gave a painful little tug at his wing, and, dropping the feather into the old man's hand, said, "Two, please."

As the coach passed on the skylark felt a little guilty, but he enjoyed the feast, and was pleased to find afterwards that no one noticed the missing feather.

The next day he flew with his father. "My son," said the old skylark, as they rose higher and higher, far above the tops of the tallest trees in the forest, "my son, I think we skylarks should be the happiest of birds. We have such brave wings. See how they lift us up into the sky, nearer and nearer unto God."

"Yes," said the young one, "Y—es . . ." But all the time he was watching a tiny speck which crept like a black beetle far below on the forest track, and he thought: "There, I've missed the coach."

The following day he waited, close to the cart-worn track. When he heard the bell ringing, he plucked another feather. It came out so easily, he pulled two more after it. Then he heard a hoarse voice shouting:

> "Who will buy? Who will buy?
> Surely we can come to terms,
> In exchange for skylark's feathers
> I am selling luscious worms."

"Three here," said the skylark.

"Very good, son, very good indeed. That will be six worms: and here's an extra one for luck," added the old man with a chuckle.

"My word," thought the young skylark, "that's a bargain." So the gay young skylark became a regular customer.

He found after a bit that he could not fly so high, but he did not mind greatly. There was less fear of the coach passing without being seen. But one day when his wings seemed thin and worn and ragged, he suddenly felt that he had been making a terrible mistake. He tried to fly up into the warm sunshine, but he fell back to the earth, like a stone.

Then he had an idea. He thought, "Dear me, of course! Why did I not think of it before! I know what I'll do. I will dig for worms and trade for feathers." Day and night he diligently searched and gathered and stored. Then he hid himself in the tall grass, waiting for the coach to pass without being seen. Soon he heard it, and again he stepped in front of the coach, saying, "Please sir, I want to know how many feathers you will trade me for all of these worms?"

Then the coachman laughed and set off at once, saying over his shoulder, "Worms for feathers is my business, not feathers for worms."

So the young skylark died and was buried under the green grass. And now they say that every summer the older birds take the young birds and fly mournfully about the grave, calling one to another as they fly:

> "Here lies a foolish skylark,
>   Hush your note each bird that sings,
> Here lies a poor lost skylark,
>   Who for earthworms sold his wings."

POEM: "The Body, Lord, Is Ours to Keep" [110]

> The body, Lord, is ours to keep
>   In glowing health and strength for Thee,
> That through its life Thy life may live,
>   Thy will move strong and swift and free;
> My body, Lord, is Thine to keep,
>   Strong and swift and free.
>
> The mind, O Lord, is ours to keep
>   In cleanliness and purity,
> That every thought and word and deed
>   May own itself akin to Thee;

My mind, O Lord, is Thine to keep,
Clean and pure and free.

The soul, O Lord, is ours to keep
In close companionship with Thee,
That soul is body, mind, and heart,
All these are but a unity;
My soul, O Lord, is Thine to keep
In comradeship with Thee.

—ELEANOR B. STOCK.

SCRIPTURE:

Watch and pray, that ye enter not into temptation: the spirit indeed is willing, but the flesh is weak.[111]

LITANY OF SUPPLICATION:

Leader: For health and strength and vigor of youth,
Response: We thank Thee, our Father.
Leader: Help us to keep our bodies strong by controlling our appetites and desires and guarding against all intemperance.
Response: Hear our prayer, our Father.
Leader: Grant that we may think of our bodies as holy temples dedicated to Thy service.
Response: Hear our prayer, our Father.
Leader: Help us to keep our minds clean and pure, thinking only thoughts that are worthy of our best selves.
Response: Hear our prayer, our Father.
Leader: In the sterner battles of life, give unto us the courage always to do the right,
Response: We humbly pray, our Father.
Leader: Inspire us with a greater desire to do Thy will,
Response: We pray Thee, O God.
Leader: Grant that we may keep our bodies fit for Thy use, and may Thy purpose for us be realized in our lives,
Response: In Jesus name, we pray. AMEN.

HYMN: *"Now in the Days of Youth."*[112]

BENEDICTION:

Dismiss us with thy blessing, and may we go forth from here to love and serve Thee with all the strength and vigor of our youth. AMEN.

Services for Intermediates

SERVICE XXXIII: LIFE THROUGH GIVING

AIM: To awaken a desire for more generous giving, not only of one's possessions, but of oneself.

PRELUDE: Music to Hymn Tune, *"Vesper Hymn."*

CALL TO WORSHIP:

> O worship the King, all-glorious above,
> O gratefully sing His power and His love;
> Our Shield and Defender, the Ancient of Days,
> Pavilioned in splendor, and girded with praise.

PRAYER HYMN:

> Holy Spirit, Truth divine,
> Dawn upon this soul of mine;
> Word of God, and inward Light,
> Wake my spirit, clear my sight.

> Holy Spirit, Love divine,
> Glow within this heart of mine;
> Kindle every high desire;
> Perish self in Thy pure fire.
> —SAMUEL LONGFELLOW.

SCRIPTURE READING:

Every good gift and every perfect gift is from above, coming down from the Father.

Freely ye have received, freely give.

Give, and it shall be given unto you; good measure, pressed down and running over, for with what measure ye mete it shall be measured to you again.

I beseech you, brethren, by the mercies of God, that ye present your bodies a living sacrifice, holy, acceptable unto God, which is your reasonable service. And be not conformed to this world: but be ye transformed by the renewing of your mind, that ye may prove what is that good, and acceptable, and perfect will of God.[113]

HYMN: *"Breathe on Me, Breath of God,"* or
"Just As I Am, Thine Own to Be."

POEM: *"I Would Live My Life"* [114]

I would live my life as the growing oak
That reaches for star and sun,
And meets its death with a lightning stroke
When its growing time is done.

I would live my life as a forest fire
That warms the earth and sky,
And takes its way with a wild desire
Up the mountains steep and high.

I would live my life as a turgid stream
That blends with the breathing sea,
And mingle my soul and love and dream
With God's infinity.

—CHAUNCEY R. PIETY.

STORY:

"THE YOUNG OAK TREE" [115]

A YOUNG oak tree was growing tall and strong and bearing with great pride its first crop of acorns, when one day it heard a bramble talking.

"These forest trees, you must know," it said, "are our greatest enemies. Look at the space they occupy. Look at the amount of nourishment they take from the earth, nourishment that by rights should be ours. Cumberers of the ground, I call them, usurpers . . ."

"Oh, but see what beautiful shade they give!" said some moss growing at the foot of a parent oak. "How cool and pleasant it is here and how glad the poor animals are to lie down in the heat of the day and find shelter from the glare. Even the birds build their nests in the branches."

"O yes, very condescending, I'm sure! But I am not one for patronage of that sort. All I know is, they absorb far more than their share of food and sunshine and spread themselves out as if the world belonged to them. Cut them down, I say, and let the poor bushes have a chance."

"You forget all the acorns they give," said another voice; "the squirrels love them and so do the pigs. The oak tree gives them freely and for nothing."

"Ah, there you are, 'for nothing'! Charity! Who wants charity, I should like to know? Besides, if it comes to that, brambles 'give' blackberries, but they prick all they can in return. I don't believe in giving anything for nothing."

Now the oak tree listened very attentively and soon began to ask itself, "Why should I give away my acorns? Why should I shelter all these creatures? What do they do for me in return?"

It grew discontented when the pigs came grunting with satisfaction to gobble up the acorns, or the squirrels ran off with one to add to their winter hoard. And when the tired horses and cows rested beneath its branches, it said, "What impertinence! I won't be made use of. Why should I?"

And slowly, slowly, its sap turned to poison and gradually dried up. No longer did the branches sway joyously in the breeze and the leaves rustle and make music. The seasons came and went, but the oak tree shrank into itself and withered. The wind sighed and the trees around waved their arms sadly to and fro and murmured, "Give! give! or how shall you receive? Bless, or there is no room for blessing!"

But the oak tree still murmured to itself, "Why should I?" It was already rotten at the core and you may see it dead any day up in the woods.

Prayer:

O Master of us all, grant that we may not seek to be comforted, but rather to comfort others; not so much to be understood, but to understand; not to be loved, but to love, for we realize that it is in giving that we really receive. Thou hast given us the good things of life with a lavish hand; we would ask for but one more gift—a grateful heart.

May we strive to be more worthy of all the good things which come from thee. In Jesus' name we pray. AMEN.

OFFERING:

Response (to be sung):

> Bless Thou the gifts our hands have brought;
> Bless Thou the work our hearts have planned;
> Ours is the faith, the will, the thought;
> The rest, O God, is in Thy hand.
> —SAMUEL LONGFELLOW.

HYMN: *"O God, Who Workest Hitherto."*

BENEDICTION:

So teach us to number our days, that we may apply our hearts unto wisdom. AMEN.

Services for Intermediates

SERVICE XXXIV: AS A MAN THINKETH

AIM: To help the group to realize the influence of thought upon action, and to lead to a greater love of the finer things in life—the beautiful, the noble, and the true.

INSTRUMENTAL PRELUDE: Music to hymn tune, *"Mercy"* (GOTTSCHALK).

CALL TO WORSHIP:

> Let us with a gladsome mind
> Praise the Lord, for He is kind:
> For His mercies aye endure,
> Ever faithful, ever sure.
>
> Let us, then, His praise sing forth,
> His high majesty and worth:
> For His mercies aye endure,
> Ever faithful, ever sure.
> —JOHN MILTON.

SUPPLICATION:

> Another day is dawning,
> Dear Master, let it be,
> In working or in waiting,
> Another day with Thee.
>
> Another day of mercies,
> Of faithfulness and grace;
> Another day of gladness
> In the shining of Thy face.

Another day of progress,
Another day of praise,
Another day of proving
Thy presence all the days.

Another day of service,
Of witness for Thy love;
Another day of training
For holier work above. [116]
—FRANCES R. HAVERGAL.

SCRIPTURE:

Consider the lilies of the fields,
How they grow;
They toil not, neither do they spin;
And yet I say unto you, That even Solomon in all his glory
was not arrayed like one of these.
When I consider thy heavens, the work of thy fingers,
The moon and the stars, which thou hast ordained;
What is man, that thou art mindful of him?
And the son of man, that thou visitest him?
For thou hast made him a little lower than the angels,
And hast crowned him with glory and honor.
Thou madest him to have dominion over the works of thy
hands;
Thou hast put all things under his feet:
All sheep and oxen, yea, and the beasts of the field;
The fowl of the air, and the fish of the sea,
And whatsoever passeth through the paths of the seas.
O Lord our Lord, how excellent is thy name in all the
earth! [117]

HYMN: *"For the Beauty of the Earth."*

RESPONSIVE READING:

Leader: And when he had called all the people unto him, he said unto
them, Hearken unto me every one of you, and understand.

Response: There is nothing from without a man, that entering into
him can defile him: but the things which come out of him, those
are they that defile the man.

Leader: A good man out of the good treasure of his heart bringeth forth that which is good; and an evil man out of the evil treasure of his heart bringeth forth that which is evil.

Response: For of the abundance of the heart his mouth speaketh.

Leader: Seek ye the Lord while he may be found, call ye upon him while he is near:

Response: Let the wicked forsake his way, and the unrighteous man his thoughts:

Leader: And let him return unto the Lord, and he will have mercy upon him; and to our God, for he will abundantly pardon.

Response: For my thoughts are not your thoughts, neither are your ways my ways, saith the Lord.

Leader: For as the heavens are higher than the earth, so are my ways higher than your ways, and my thoughts than your thoughts.

Response: Commit thy works unto the Lord, and thy thoughts shall be established.[118]

HYMN: *"Fairest Lord Jesus,"* or
"O Young and Fearless Prophet of Ancient Galilee."

STORY:

"WHAT THE BUTTERFLY LEARNED" [119]

HE WAS a beautiful, big butterfly with great golden wings. And he was such a happy butterfly, too. He just flew around here, and there, and everywhere. When he grew tired of flying, he settled down on a twig and swung lazily back and forth until he was rested. If he were thirsty, he dipped down his head and took a drop of dew from a leaf. If he were hungry, he dug down deep into a blossom and got a taste of the honey it contained.

One day as the butterfly was flying about, he happened to notice below him some very beautiful things, scattered here and there on the ground. It was a brilliant multicolored expanse—yellow, red, purple, and pink. The bright beauty of the object beneath him aroused his curiosity because he could not understand why anything possessing so much loveliness should be content to remain in one place.

The butterfly thought about this for quite a while, and finally decided to go down and talk to some of those brightly colored things. So he flew a long way until he came to a hillside that was covered with flowers, as far as he could see. Each flower had ever so many white petals—long, slender, and pointed—growing out from a big, yellow center.

The butterfly went down very close to the one great big flower and whispered in her ear: "Daisy, why don't you fly about as I do? Don't you get tired of sitting here so still?"

"Oh, no," said the Daisy; "I have a good time here. If I get tired in the heat of the day, I wait until night comes, and then I look up at the sky and watch the stars come out. I love the stars. I think they are the most beautiful things in the world, and I wish I were like them."

"Why, Daisy," said the butterfly, "you are like the stars!" Then the daisy was as happy as could be, and the butterfly flew away.

After a while he saw beneath him what seemed to be a big blue blanket over the grass, but when he came near he found it wasn't a blanket at all, but a big patch of little blue flowers.

He flew close to one of the blue flowers and spoke very softly. "Forget-me-not, why do you sit so still all day long? Don't you get tired?"

"Oh, no, I don't get tired at all," said the Forget-me-not in a very soft voice. "I just sit here all day long and look up at the sky. I think there is nothing in all the world so wonderful as the beautiful blue sky. I love it and I wish I were like it."

"Why, you are like the blue sky, Forget-me-not!" exclaimed the butterfly. And the forget-me-not was as happy as could be, so the butterfly flew away.

He traveled a long distance, and then he found a flower growing by the roadside. It grew on a tall, stiff stem. Its petals were bright yellow, round, and shiny, and each blossom looked like a cup.

The butterfly said to the buttercup, "Why do you sit here so still all day long? You must get very tired. Don't you ever fly around as I do?"

Then the buttercup shook her little head, and said, "Oh, I just love to see all the people as they drive by, and I watch the boys and girls as they go to school. I never tire of sitting here and looking at the sun, the great big splendid sun. I just love the sun, and I wish I were like it."

"Why, this is the strangest thing," answered the butterfly. "You are very like the sun, Buttercup, for you are round, yellow, and shining." And the buttercup was as happy as could be, so the butterfly flew away.

By this time the butterfly was growing very tired, so he flew down to a quiet spot to rest awhile. He settled down beside a little stream, where the grass, trees, and vines made it very inviting. He didn't really expect to find any flowers there, but nestled in the grass was a little purple flower, such a modest little flower. It almost seemed to hang its head when he spoke to it.

"Violet," said the butterfly, "why do you stay here so still in this one place? Why don't you fly around? Aren't you ever tired?"

"Yes," said the violet, "I do sometimes get tired during the long hours of the day; but when I do, I just wait patiently until the twilight. I love the colors that come in the sky when the sun sets. I love them all, but the purple is the most beautiful of all. I just love it, and I wish I were like it."

The butterfly was quiet a moment, and then he spoke very softly: "Why, little Violet, you are exactly like the purple that comes in the sky when the sun sets." The violet was as happy as could be. Then the butterfly flew away.

That night the shadows grew long and gradually darkness settled down over the earth. All the little flowers folded their petals and swayed quietly to and fro until they were fast asleep, and each little flower was as happy as could be, because it was like the thing it loved. And the great big brown butterfly thought to himself: "Isn't it wonderful! It seems that in this world everyone grows to be like the thing he loves. One watches a loved object and thinks about it until he finally grows to be like it."

Directed Meditation:

When we see the beauty about us are we aware that God is seeking to reveal Himself to us through his handiwork? He is trying to speak to us through the beauty of nature. What message comes to us as we think of the universe which God has created? . . . [Pause.] The flowers do not bloom for themselves, but for our enjoyment. The song of the birds, the beauty of the sunset, the soft glow of the moonlight—all these are gifts from God's hand for our pleasure . . . [Pause.] Are we able to fully appreciate and enter into this heritage which is rightfully ours? . . . [Pause.] What kind of a Creator is back of all these bountiful gifts? . . . [Pause.]

As we think of the peace and harmony in nature, help us to live calm and serene lives. Forgive our foolish ways and help us to center our thoughts on the beautiful, the good, and the true. Grant that we may commit our ways unto Thee, trusting in Thy wisdom to guide us. In Jesus' name we pray. AMEN.

BENEDICTION:

So teach us to number our days, that we may apply our hearts unto wisdom. AMEN.

SERVICE XXXV: CLEANNESS OF THOUGHT

AIM: To lead the group to consider the importance of worthy motives, clean thinking, and clean living.

INSTRUMENTAL PRELUDE: *"Prayer,"* Op. 48, No. 1 (BEETHOVEN).

CALL TO WORSHIP:

Leader: The hour cometh, and now is, when the true worshipers shall worship the Father in spirit and in truth;

Response: For the Father seeketh such to worship him.

Leader: Let us worship the Lord in the beauty of holiness.

Response: Accept our worship, we pray.

Leader: Let us lift up our hearts unto the Almighty and Eternal Creator who lives in all that is pure and gracious.

Response: We lift up grateful hearts, our Father.

PRAYER:

"Give Us, O Father" [120]

Give us, O Father,
　Hearts that are new,
Faith that is daring,
　Love that is true,
Farseeing vision,
　Big as the race,
Teach us to serve thee,
　Each in his place.

Give us, O Father,
　Thoughts that are pure,

Hope that is noble,
   Truth that is sure,
Motives unselfish,
   Minds that are free;
Lead us and teach us
   More about thee.

Give us, O Father,
   Dreams that are fair,
High aspirations,
   Ideals to share,
Strength for achievement,
   Courage to be—
Live in our living,
   Make us like thee.
                    —CHAUNCEY R. PIETY.

SCRIPTURE READING (in unison):

O Lord, thou hast searched me, and known me.
For there is not a word in my tongue, but, lo,
O Lord, thou knowest it altogether.
Whither shall I go from thy spirit?
Or whither shall I flee from thy presence?
If I take the wings of the morning,
And dwell in the uttermost parts of the sea;
Even there shall thy hand lead me,
And thy right hand shall hold me.
Search me, O God, and know my heart:
Try me, and know my thoughts:
And see if there be any wicked way in me,
And lead me in the way everlasting.

The steps of a good man are ordered by the Lord;
And he delighteth in his way.
The law of the Lord is in his heart;
None of his steps shall slide.
Mark the perfect man, and behold the upright:
For the end of that man is peace.
Blessed are the pure in heart:
For they shall see God.[121]

Hymn: *"Purer Yet and Purer,"* or
"Gracious Spirit, Dwell with Me."

Story:

"PURITY IS DEARER THAN LIFE" [122]

In the forests of northern Europe and Asia there lives a little animal called the ermine. Because of his snow-white fur, he is considered the most beautiful of animals, and yields one of the most valuable of commercial furs. Ermine is used for neckpieces, muffs, and trimmings of various garments. It is also used to line the robes of kings, queens, and judges of England. The pure white of the fur has made it a symbol of purity, a quality usually associated with the office of a judge.

The best skins are taken in the extremely cold sections of northern Russia, Norway, Sweden, and Canada. The color of the fur is affected greatly by the climate. From a reddish brown it turns to a yellowish white in moderate weather, and to a pure white in intense cold, but the very tip of the tail is always black.

The ermine lives in thickets and in stony places; and, frequently, makes use of deserted homes of moles and other underground mammals.

Trapping requires great patience and exposure to bitterly cold weather; consequently, few skins are taken yearly. Since an ordinary trap would tear the soft silky fur, other means must be used to catch this wary little creature.

The ermine has a peculiar pride in his white coat, and at all hazards protects it from anything that would soil it. So the fur hunters take cruel advantage of this little animal's desire to keep his coat clean. They do not set a trap to take him at some unwary moment, but, instead, they find his home—a cleft in a rock or a hollow tree—and daub the entrance and interior with repulsive dirt. The dogs then start the chase. Frightened, the little ermine flees for his home—his only place of refuge. When he reaches it, he finds it daubed with filth and will not enter for fear of soiling his pure white coat.

Rather than go into the unclean place, the ermine faces the yelping dogs and preserves the purity of his fur at the price of his life. It is better that his coat be stained with blood than soiled with dirt. This instinct for cleanliness leads him to regard his white fur as his

dearest possession, and he keeps it clean regardless of what happens
He has only a white coat, but he gives his life to keep it spotless.

POEM: *"God, Who Touchest Earth with Beauty"* [123]

God, who touchest earth with beauty,
Make me lovely too,
With Thy Spirit re-create me,
Make my heart anew.

Like thy springs and running waters,
Make me crystal pure,
Like thy rocks of towering grandeur,
Make me strong and sure.

Like thy dancing waves in sunlight,
Make me glad and free,
Like the straightness of the pine trees,
Let me upright be.

Like the arching of the heavens,
Lift my thoughts above,
Turn my dreams to noble action,
Ministries of love.

God, who touchest earth with beauty,
Make me lovely too,
Keep me ever, by Thy Spirit,
Pure and strong and true.
—MARY S. EDGAR.

PRAYER:

Our Father, help us to realize that if we would live by the stand-
ards which Jesus set, we must guard against unclean thoughts or unworthy motives. Grant that we may make our decisions in such a
way that there will be nothing in our lives to hide from the world.
Help us to realize that purity is dearer than life; and may we hold on
to it regardless of what happens.

"We would affirm our faith in life and call life good and not evil.
We accept the limitations of our own life and believe it is possible for
us to live a beautiful and Christlike life within the conditions set for
us. Through the power of Christ which descends on us, and which

dwells in our spirit, we know that we can be more than conquerors through Christ our Lord." [124] AMEN.

HYMN: *"I Would Be True."*

BENEDICTION:

Now unto him that is able to keep you from falling, and to present you faultless before the presence of his glory; to God the Father, be glory and majesty, dominion and power, both now and forever more. AMEN.

GROUP VII

Services for Intermediates

SERVICE XXXVI: SHARING

AIM: To lead to an awareness that the measure of our love to God is the extent of our service to our fellow man.

INSTRUMENTAL PRELUDE: Music to hymn tune, *"Finlandia."*

CALL TO WORSHIP:

Leader:

> Wait on the Lord: be of good courage,
> And He shall strengthen thy heart.

Response:

> The Lord is my light and my salvation;
> Whom shall I fear?
> The Lord is the strength of my life;
> Of whom shall I be afraid?

HYMN: *"Spirit of God, Descend upon My Heart."*

SCRIPTURE READING:

Then came to him the mother of Zebedee's children with her sons, worshiping him, and desiring a certain thing of him. And he said unto her, What wilt thou? She saith unto him, Grant that these my two sons may sit, the one on thy right hand, and the other on thy left, in thy kingdom. But Jesus answered and said, Ye know not what ye ask. Are ye able to drink of the cup that I shall drink of, and to be baptized with the baptism that I am baptized with? They say unto him, We are able. And he said unto them, Ye shall drink indeed of my cup, and be baptized with the baptism that I am baptized with: but to sit on my right hand, and on my left, is not mine to give, but it shall be given to them for whom it is prepared of my Father. And when the ten heard it, they were moved with indignation against the two brethren. But Jesus called them unto him, and said, Ye know that the princes of the Gentiles exercise dominion over them, and they that are great exercise authority upon them. But it shall not be so among you: but whosoever will be great among you, let him be your minister; and whosoever will be chief among you, let him be your servant: even as the Son of man came not to be ministered unto, but to minister, and to give his life a ransom for many.[125]

STORY:

"THE WHITE FIRE" [126]

THREE MEN CAME to Love the Lord, asking a gift of his white fire, and the gift was not denied. "Take it, keep it, use it!" said Love the Lord; and they answered joyfully, "Yea, Lord, this will we do!"

Then the three fared forth on their way, the old way, the new way, and the only way; yet they went not together, but each by himself alone.

Presently one came to a dark valley, full of men who groped with their hands, seeking the way, and finding it not, for they had no light; and they moaned, and cried, "O! that we had light to show us the way!"

Then that man answered aloud, "Yes, and there shall be light!"

And he took the fire that was given him of Love the Lord, and made of it a torch, and held it aloft, and it flashed through the darkness like a sword, and showed the way; and with him leading, they followed, and came safely through that place into the light of day.

The second man went by another path of the way, and it led him over a bleak moor, where the wind blew bitter keen, and the rocks stood like frozen iron; and here were men shivering with cold, huddling together for warmth, yet finding none, for they had no fire. And they moaned and cried, "Ah! if we had but fire to keep the life in us, for we perish!"

And the man said, "Yes, there shall be fire!"

And he took the fire that he had of Love the Lord, and spread it out, and set fagots to it, and it blazed up broad and bright; and the folk gathered round it, and held their hands and warmed themselves at it, and forgot the bitter wind.

Now the third man went his way also; and as he went he said to himself, "How shall I keep my fire safe, that no fierce wind blow it out, and no foul vapor stifle it? I know what I will do: I will hide it in my heart, and so no harm can come to it." And he hid the fire in his heart, and carried it so and went on.

Now by and by those three came to the end of the way, and there waited for them one in white, and his face veiled. He said to the first man, "What of your fire?"

And the man said, "I found folk struggling in darkness, and I made a torch of my fire, and showed them the way; now it is well-nigh wasted, yet it still burns."

And he in white said, "It is well; this fire shall never die."

Then came the second, and of him, too, that one asked, "What of your fire?"

And he said, "I found men shivering with nought to warm them, and I gave my fire, that they might live and not die."

And he in white answered again, "It is well; this fire, too, shall never die."

Then came the third, and answered boldly, and said, "I have brought my fire safe, through peril and through strife; lo, see it here in my heart!"

Then that one in white put aside his veil; and it was Love the Lord himself. "Alas!" he said; "what is this you have done?"

And he opened the man's heart; and inside it was a black char, and white ashes lying in it.

POEM: *"I Sought His Love in Sun and Stars"* [127]

I sought His love in sun and stars,
    And where the wild seas roll;
I found it not, as mute I stood,
    Fear overwhelmed my soul;
But when I gave to one in need,
    I found the Lord of Love indeed.

I sought His love in lore of books,
    In charts of science's skill;
They left me orphaned as before—
    His love eluded still;

Then in despair I breathed a prayer—
The Lord of Love was standing there!
　　　　　　　—THOMAS CURTIS CLARK.

PRAYER:

Heavenly Father, every good and perfect gift comes from Thee, and it is of Thine own that we give to Thee. Help us to hold all our resources in trust for Thy use. May we, by means of them, create untold blessings for Thy children. Forgive us that we have ever exploited others for our gain instead of expressing to them Thy love. Through Jesus Christ our Lord. AMEN.[128]

HYMN: *"The Light of God Is Falling."* [129]

BENEDICTION:

The Lord mercifully with His favor look upon you, and fill you with all spiritual benedictions and grace; that in this life, and in the world to come, ye may be partakers of eternal life. AMEN.

APPENDIX

ADDITIONAL STORIES
BIBLIOGRAPHY
REFERENCE AND NOTES
INDEX OF STORIES
INDEX OF HYMNS

A KIND-HEARTED JAPANESE [139]

IN THE EARLY DAYS of Japan, savage tribes lived in the island of Formosa. These savage men wanted to worship God, but they had very queer ideas about what would be pleasing to God. They believed that a great and powerful God would want his worshipers to do in his honor the most dangerous and difficult thing they knew how to do—that thing, according to their idea, was to hunt and kill other men. In order to show honor and praise to God, they would hunt men, cut off their heads, and hang them in the temple for God to see. Every year, just before their great religious festival, bands of savages organized hunting parties and searched for men whom they could kill— the heads were brought back and dedicated to God. This practice continued for many years.

About two hundred years ago Goho, a wise and good man, became the chief of the tribe of Ari. This tribe lived in the very center of Formosa, at Mount Ari, which is now famous for "Hinoki" or Japanese cypress. Goho was a kind-hearted man. He could not believe that God wanted men's heads dedicated to him, so he resolved that while he was chief he would put an end to the terrible practice of head-hunting.

Because Goho was a kind man, he had done many helpful things for the members of his tribe, and they loved and honored him as if he were their father. The year he became chief, forty heads were brought in by the head-hunters. When Goho suggested that they dedicate only one head a year and put the others away for future years, they agreed to the plan. He hoped that in forty years they would forget the savage joy of head-hunting and consent to give up the practice.

At the end of the forty years there was no head to be dedicated to God on the day of the great religious festival. Goho hoped no one would think of it, but a few days before the festival a group of savage men came and begged Goho to allow them to go head-hunting again. Wise, kind Goho talked with the men long and earnestly and told them it was not a good thing to kill men and not pleasing to God to have heads dedicated to him—so he persuaded them to try celebrating the festival without dedicating a head.

Each year he persuaded them to wait another year—until four years had passed. Then the savages grew restless and could not be persuaded again. So Goho said to them, "If you must have a head to dedicate, you are to kill the man I select." The savages agreed to that. A few days later he sent them word that all was ready. The head-hunters must hide behind the temple and watch for a man wearing a red cap and dressed in red clothes. If he passed before the door of the temple just before noon, they could kill him and cut off his head.

With eager anticipation the band of armed warriors came to the temple and hid behind a jutting tower. They watched the sun as it climbed higher and higher. They argued as to who should have the privilege of cutting off the head, and finally drew lots for the honor. As the sun neared the zenith they grew still and tense. Presently, in the distance they saw a flash of red. Each man grasped his bow and fitted his arrow to the string. Slowly the figure dressed in red came nearer, his head bowed so that they could not see his face. Just as he stood in front of the temple door a cloud of arrows came flying through the air and pierced his body in a dozen places. He fell face down mortally wounded. The savages rushed from their hiding place with drawn blades; the chosen man cut off the head and lifted it up for all to see.

All eyes turned toward the bleeding head. When the pale face came into view, there was deathlike stillness; then a wail of horror and despair, for they recognized the features of their dearly beloved chief, Goho. They bitterly repented what they had done—and bowing before the head of Goho, they pledged themselves never to hunt heads again. They built a shrine to the spirit of Goho and lived true to their pledge. Two hundred years have passed, but still men of Ari refuse to join the other tribes in the gruesome practice of head-hunting.

THE TOILING OF FELIX [131]

ONCE UPON A TIME in far-away Egypt there lived a young man whose name was Felix. Though his country still clung to its old religion, Felix was a Christian. As he read the stories in the Bible about Jesus and the way men loved and followed him about, Felix began to long to see the face of Jesus; he felt that it would make him supremely happy to see Jesus—if only one time.

His entire life became a search to learn how he might see the face of Christ. He spent years reading old books where many beliefs about Jesus were written. Then he began a pilgrimage to all the beautiful churches and temples; he spent weeks praying at these shrines, hoping for a glimpse of the Christ. He shut himself in a silent room and kept vigil night and day. Day by day he dropped the duties of everyday life and broke his ties with friends and family. His only thought was for his own purpose, his own happiness. He thought that if he gave up his love for everything and everybody in this world, surely Jesus would come into his life—but his search was in vain.

He grew discouraged and was ready to give up in despair. He made another earnest prayer and felt that he was urged to keep on seeking. He heard of a holy man who lived as a hermit on a mountaintop. He resolved to go to the hermit with the hope that the holy man could help him in his search. Long and toilsome was his journey with Egypt's blazing sun above him and blistering sands beneath his feet. Patiently he plodded onward till he reached the mountaintop. There he found the holy man had shut himself within a cave. Bands of pilgrims, who came seeking a blessing from the saint, brought him food.

Month by month the hermit dwelt in seclusion, fasting, and praying. Only once a year did he leave his cave. On that day he gave a special favor to some one person in the band of pilgrims. Felix knelt at the door of the cave and begged the hermit to speak and tell him how to find the Christ, but there was no response.

So Felix waited in patience until the day when the hermit would appear. He made his home in an old tomb near the pilgrim's road. There the faithful pilgrims saw him waiting without complaint and learned to call him holy and fed him as they did the hermit.

At last the day dawned when the hermit would make his gift. Felix knelt before the hermit's door and hardly dared to lift his eyes. The cavern door opened and the hermit stood a moment and placed his hands upon Felix's head, blessing him without a word, then he placed in Felix's hand a strange gift—a torn fragment of an old papyrus book. Eagerly Felix read its message, seeking a way to find the Christ. Here are the words he found upon that ancient bit of paper: "Raise the stone, and thou shalt find me; cleave the wood, and there am I."

Disappointed and heavy-hearted, Felix made his way down the mountain wondering if the Christ for whom he had searched so long really spoke these words. Could it be possible that Jesus wanted men to seek him through toil among the rocks and trees? The words kept ringing through his mind, "Raise the stone, and thou shalt find me; cleave the wood, and there am I."

As he neared the foot of the mountain he saw the shining surface of a broad river. Then he heard clanking hammers and clinking drills in a nearby quarry. With a last look at the mountaintop he turned and made his way through the dust and noise of the quarry. After his months of quietness and prayer far from the haunts of man, this place of work seemed a Babel of hot confusion.

Felix asked for a job and was soon swinging a huge mallet to drive an iron wedge into the rock. The ringing blows were shocks to his sensitive nerves; his long unused muscles quivered and his head throbbed with pain. Day after day he toiled, learning to use willow wedges to split the rocks, helping with chains and rollers to carry huge stone blocks to the riverside.

As Felix worked side by side with his fellow workmen, he learned to love the labor and to love the men. Every day he grew stronger and felt happier, knowing that he had done his part. He no longer dreamed of being a hermit saint, but watched with pride as the stones were carried across the river to build a city.

As he looked at the distant city, temples, houses, domes, and towers, he cried in exultation: "All that mighty work is ours, every worker in the quarry, every builder in the city is in the regiment of

God," for he had come to realize that "honest toil is holy service, faithful work is praise and prayer."

As he lived and worked with the men in the quarry, he grew to feel that they were a real brotherhood—he cheered them with his singing, he told them stories of Jesus, and taught them how to pray. He was ever ready to lend a helping hand when needed. One day a comrade fainted from the heat, and Felix brought palm leaves to shelter him and cool water to bathe his face. As he leaned over the fainting workman in kindly sympathy and helpfulness, a strange radiance seemed to fill the place, and Felix caught a fleeting look of Jesus' face.

On another day, a rafstman slipped and fell into the river. Felix plunged in to rescue him. As he struggled to carry the man's weight against the cruel current of the river, he wondered if his strength would be sufficient to reach the shore. In this time of sore distress, he seemed to see One beside him walking on the waves. Did he dream it or was it true?

At last the labor was over, and Felix made his way to the city his hands had helped to build. There again he went into the temple and knelt at the altar in prayer.

"I have done thy bidding, Master; raised the rock and felled the tree. This I know: Thou hast been near me. I love thee, though I cannot see thee. Let me do thy humblest task!" Through the temple slowly spread a mystic light—and there stood the Master, his hands showing the signs of labor, and his face bearing the marks of care. These simple words he spoke to Felix: "They who toil and labor follow the path my feet have trod. And they who work willingly do the will of God. Every deed of love and mercy is done to me. You need not seek any more, for I am with you everywhere. Raise the stone, and thou shalt find me; cleave the wood, and there am I."

WHEN YOU make a trip around the world you will find in India many things of interest because of their beauty or because of their great antiquity. For instance, you will be sure to notice queer stone towers, some one hundred feet high crowned with three or more stone umbrellas. These towers are called "stupas," and in the great cities they are enormous structures three or four hundred feet in height and one hundred feet in diameter. When you ask questions about these queer towers that you see in so many places, the people of India will tell you that they were built by a king who reigned two hundred sixty-four years before Christ. They may suggest that you make a pilgrimage following the path of King Asoka's pilgrimage so that you can see his story carved on the hillsides near the main-traveled roads of the country. For pilgrimages have been the custom in India since the days of this great king.

It would be a novel adventure to travel over the roads that have been worn by the feet of millions of men for thousands of years, and to read history from carved rocks in the hillsides instead of from books. It would be possible to follow King Asoka's path because he built the queer towers to mark his pilgrimage. Even if you do not have the rare adventure of walking over the same road that Asoka traveled, you can remember his story and you may have experiences very much like his.

There were hundreds of kings who ruled over India before and since the coming of Christ. We do not know their names or anything about their lives. It is because Asoka lived such an unusual life, because he did something no king had done before, that he is remembered today.

When King Asoka was a young boy he loved to listen to the stories of the old men who knew his grandfather. They told thrilling tales of the days when Alexander the Great invaded their kingdom and captured many of their cities and provinces. His eyes flashed with pride when the storytellers described his grandfather as a bold young warrior who led victorious armies to recapture the lost cities. Asoka determined to be a great warrior when he became a man; so he practiced diligently in the use of bow and arrow, the sword, and other implements of war.

Asoka grew to be a strong and splendid man. His keen mind, his commanding voice and manner won the admiration and loyalty of all his subjects. He looked every inch a king, and he loved to go along the highways riding in his gold palanquin at the head of a gorgeous procession. His chief pleasure and pastime was hunting wild animals. He did this on a grand scale, too. When he went forth to hunt the streets were roped off to protect his route. Men with drums and gongs led the procession, while beautiful women on horseback or in chariots surrounded Asoka's palanquin. These women were very swift and skillful in the use of bows and arrows and brought down many animals in the chase.

When Asoka became king he gave his attention to building up a great army. His ambition to be a soldier grew stronger. He became a skillful leader and extended his empire by conquering many small surrounding kingdoms. His ambition grew with his success, and he planned to take his conquering army to far-away Greece, the land of Alexander the Great, who had invaded his grandfather's kingdom.

To carry out his great ambition to conquer Greece and build a world empire, he began careful preparation. He laid heavy taxes on all the subject kingdoms and enlisted large armies. He spent his days interviewing travelers who could tell him of the land and water routes which his armies would have to cross. His ambition spread throughout his armies; interest and excitement ran high.

One day as King Asoka traveled along the highway his attention was attracted by a man sitting in quiet meditation beneath a tree. His face looked so calm and happy, Asoka wondered if he had some secret source of pleasure. He sent for the man to come and ride with him in his gold palanquin so that he might learn his secret. King Asoka and the stranger had a long and earnest conversation. The stranger drew from his robe a parchment scroll and gave it to the king, then returned to sit in quiet meditation under the tree.

For days King Asoka pored over the writing on the scroll, then laid aside his jewelry and gorgeous robes and, clad in simple garments, spent days sitting under a tree in meditation. When his generals came to report that all was ready for the campaign to invade Greece and begin a world empire, he smiled and shook his head. Then he told them that he had entered on the path of true knowledge and that he had made very different plans.

Consternation and keen disappointment spread among the young soldiers. The king's closest friends tried to argue with him; they described his waiting army as the finest in the world. They painted alluring pictures of the glorious victories he would win; they urged him to realize his ambition to be emperor of the world. His only answer was to turn back to the scroll and read again what was written thereon.

And what was this scroll that had wrought such a change in King Asoka's plans? It was an account of the life and teaching of Gautama, a wise and good man who had lived two hundred and fifty years before. Gautama is called the Buddha because the word *buddha* means "The Enlightened One." Gautama taught that the good life, the way to be happy and to please God, was to live simply, be kind and helpful to your fellow men, to seek wisdom and understanding through prayer and meditation—which was very different from the pleasure-loving, warlike life of King Asoka. But King Asoka had chosen, to use his own words, "the path of true knowledge."

Just as the Roman emperor, Constantine the Great, hundreds of years later, embraced the Christian faith and swung his whole empire into Christianity, so King Asoka, when he learned the teachings of Buddha, wanted all his subjects to learn to live the good life. So, instead of leading an army to kill and conquer, he led a peaceful procession of his followers on a pilgrimage throughout his kingdom. As the carved histories on the hillsides tell us, "Instead of the sound of the war drum, the sound of the drum of piety is heard, while heavenly spectacles of processional cars, elephants, illuminations, and the like are displayed to the people." And everywhere he and his messengers went he had them build the queer stone towers sheltered by the stone umbrellas. On the walls of the towers were inscribed the teachings of Buddha, so that all men could read them. And on these tours, the records say, money was distributed to the poor and religious instruction and teachings were carried on.

King Asoka devoted his life to the good of his people. He ordered that healing herbs, good for man and beast, be planted in his dominion and those adjoining. "In like manner roots and fruits have been imported and planted. On the roads trees have been planted and wells have been dug for the use of man and beast." These reforms and improvements were unheard of in the annals of other kings of that time.

He wanted to share "the path of true knowledge" with all men, so he sent his messengers to other countries. "My neighbors, too, should learn this lesson," he writes—so his good will reached even to Greece and Egypt.

While he worked so diligently to spread the teachings of the Buddha, he respected the religions of other people. There has never been a finer or more sincere statement than this one carved on the hillside in India: "His majesty does reverence to men of all sects by donations and various modes of reverence. A man must not do reverence to his own sect by disparaging that of another man for trivial reasons."

If Asoka had gone on with his wars, probably we would never have heard of him; but as a peace king he has been selected by an outstanding modern historian as one of the seven great figures of early history. We do well to honor Asoka, for he is the only war king who abandoned warfare in the midst of victory.

"GO PREACH" [133]

PICTURE INTERPRETATION

EUGENE BURNAND (1850-1921): *"Go Preach My Gospel"*

HERE is the Great Commission reduced to its simplest terms. It is a personal appeal for loyalty and service, from a great teacher to his pupil. It is not the historic Jesus of Nazareth calling Peter and John; it is the eternal Christ appealing to youth—in every land, through all the centuries. Burnand names the picture "Go Preach," but he might as well have named it "Go Teach," or "Go Sell," or "Go Paint." He has really dramatized the eternal call of God to the human heart, the eternal urge by which God drives men toward higher things. Christ is here pointing out a way of life, summoning youth to follow an ideal, to accept a companionship, to assume a task.

How does one know this?

First, observe the face and eyes of Christ. They bear the stamp of the dreamer, the idealist. The eyes are raised a little above the level of earth, and they are not converged upon an object. They are seeing things as a whole rather than in detail; the mind behind them is occupied with principles and grand objectives; and the hand, that a lesser artist would have made to point to something specific, is merely suggesting something vague, over the horizon, up in the heavens.

Next look at the young man's face. The brow is contracted; the eyes are sharply focused and converged upon a distant object. The disciple is earnestly trying to make out a specific goal, a task in time and place to which he may address himself; something to work out, accomplish. There is no vagueness in his mind about this call; there is nothing ethereal in it. He is about to tackle a "job."

This difference in the two faces is intentional. Burnand has interpreted correctly the historic and perpetual relationship between Christ and his disciples. Christ has a vision of a world redeemed, of the kingdom of God, the brotherhood of man, human nature transformed by love from selfishness to co-operation. This is a grand and compelling ideal that is indeed over the horizon and partly in the clouds, but it grips young people powerfully and sets them on fire for service. But the ideal must be worked out in practical and concrete ways.

Down through the ages young enthusiasts have picked out their specific jobs. Paul sees his task to be founding a church; Dorcas making coats for the poor at Joppa. St. Francis washes the wounds of lepers and weds Lady Poverty. Luther nails his world-shaking challenge on the church door at Wittenberg. Jane Addams brings hope to youth on the city streets. Millions down through the ages have caught the vision of God's kingdom over the horizon, in the sky, and have followed the gleam each in his own way to a definite end; and always under the inspiration of the Great Captain.

What a wonderful partnership it is! The challenge and the response, the far-off ideal and the task near at hand.

Do you notice that the left arm of Christ is around the young man's shoulder, that Christ's head bends slightly toward the young man's, and that the great red cloak covers both persons? That is the artist's way of saying: "Lo, I am with you alway"; "Having loved his own, he loved them until the end"; "What shall separate us from the love of Christ?" "I in them and Thou in me"; "I can do all things through Christ which strengtheneth me."

FROM THE TUILERIES TO THE BASTILLE

SOME PERSONS appear to be born to a career mixed with triumph and disappointments, honors and persecutions. The French artist and philosopher, Bernard Palissy, seems to be one of them. Born about 1518, his life from beginning to end is a mixture of disappointments and triumphs, but also one of courageous persistence. At Agen he learned the art of painting on glass and also something of surveying. With these arts he supported himself on a tour of France and Germany, during which time he devoted himself attentively to all the books he could secure, and acquired an extensive knowledge of the natural sciences. Returning to France, he married and settled at Saintes.

Upon seeing a beautiful enameled vase, he determined, not only to discover the enameling process, but to improve upon it. Being ignorant of the potter's art, he had to grope his way, laboring year after year without success, reducing his family to want, and almost starving himself. He did not know what chemicals would produce enamel, but he experimented with different combinations which he spread upon pieces of pottery, and baked in a furnace of his own construction. Time after time he failed, but this only made him more determined. There was no encouragement from his friends or family. His friends thought him foolish, and his wife objected because of the scarcity of money in the home. Palissy continued his experiments, building another furnace, trying other combinations, but with the same result.

Failure after failure attended his efforts, until finally there was some indication of success. He then prepared for one more effort which resulted in one piece of pottery being covered with enamel. Building a larger furnace, he determined to complete the process. This required months of labor. The first test was a failure, but one more trial brought him success. This last effort, while it brought him reward, was also tragic. As he fed his last fuel into the furnace, the enameling compound had not melted. Unmindful of everything, he began to strip the palings from the fence and feed them into the furnace. When the compound had still not melted, he turned to the furniture in his home—tables, chairs, and shelves. His wife left the house thinking he had lost his mind, but the last blast of heat had been sufficient to melt the enameling compound.

When the pieces of pottery came out of the furnace, they were a beautiful white. After more than sixteen years of experimenting, he had obtained a pure white enamel which afforded a perfect ground for the application of decorative art. Today Palissy ware, covered with jasper-white enamel, upon which animals, insects, and plants are represented in their natural forms and colors, is greatly valued and much sought after by collectors. The beautiful palace and garden of the Tuileries are known throughout the world, yet few know that they stand upon the site of Palissy's kiln, from which their name is derived.

Palissy became a prosperous potter, and one would think that his days of sorrow and distress were over. Yet such was not the case. Other and greater trials were yet ahead, but in them can be seen the stability and grandeur of the man. Early in life he became a Protestant and was very active in that faith. The recognition which he had gained as a potter saved his life on the night of the massacre of St. Bartholomew's Day. However, he could not long withstand the hatred of his enemies. He was arrested and thrown into prison. Here the moral courage of the man appeared. When freedom was offered him on the condition that he would recant, he replied: "I am glad to give my life for the glory of God." The king of France said: "I regret that I am compelled to leave you in the hands of your enemies." Palissy retorted: "They can compel you, but they cannot compel me. I know how to die." Not many days later he died in the Bastille, a martyr for his faith. In his death France lost one of the noblest souls which that country has ever produced.

THE CHAIRMAN of the Second World Conference was finishing his opening speech. He ended with a thunder of benign platitudes and then stood silent, waiting for applause. It came. So he sat down.

Then it was that the dark man, with black brows that met, got quickly to his feet. No one had seen him enter. He had a swarthy-weathered skin, as one who might have traveled far to reach the conference hall, enduring roughest trials, storms, shipwrecks. His hair had once been raven, but the years had sprinkled it with gray. He had a strong hooked nose, and eyes of blue.

His voice had a touch of roughness in it, as though he had used it much. It filled the conference hall.

"Though I speak," said he, "with the tongues of men and of angels, and have not charity, I am become as sounding brass, or a tinkling cymbal!"

The babel of the tongues of men died down.

The chairman, towering, arose. "Will the delegate address the Chair?"

"I was addressing it—especially!"

The chairman bristled. "I do not seem to know the delegate," he said. "May I ask the delegate's name?"

"Paulus," he replied. "Gaius Julius Paulus."

The conference secretary searched his list of delegates, glanced up swiftly to the chairman, and shook his head.

The chairman, reassured, indulged in heavy irony. "We have a delegate from modern Italy, but none, it happens, was invited from the ancient empire. The name you give would fit in well in the Roman world of Christ's time."

The blue-eyed man smiled. "My family goes back that far, and Roman citizens we were, though of another race—the only one without a delegate here. I am a Jew."

Some mad disturber, then. Some Hebrew fanatic. The chairman beckoned to the sergeant-at-arms. The sergeant nodded to his men.

But when they came near the sturdy thick-set man he turned his blue eyes on them.

"First I will talk," he said.

The sergeant-at-arms made no attempt to stop him. Perhaps it was magnetism, the sheer virility of the man that held them fascinated; or, perhaps, the simple beauty of his words.

"Though I speak with the tongues of men and of angels," he began again, "and have not charity. . . ."

As he spoke there was not a delegate but knew that the Second World Conference was headed for fiasco, like the first. Each man knew just why he was there—to get away with every last possible shred of advantage for his own nation. The vibrant voice was in their ears:

"Charity seeketh not her own . . ."

Out of the world assemblage not one delegate was there whose mission was to help out man in this grave hour of mutual distress. They were all plotting, scheming. Each suspected all.

"Charity thinketh no evil . . ."

Each delegate looked at all the other delegates and then, for some strange cause, looked within himself—and none took any pleasure in the things he saw. So each turned toward the speaker and listened while he told them of a medicine for the sickness of the world. They were the more ashamed because they all had known about it, and had been trying every other remedy—each of which had failed.

"Charity never faileth," continued the man. He had finished speaking and was gone. No one had seen him go. The tongues of men began to work again; but somehow there was not the sound of babel now in the great conference hall.

The delegates from America, Japan, and Russia stood in a little group. Each understood the language of the others.

"Fools!" growled the Russian. "Hating each other—Russia and Japan. Two friendly men—you, Baron Susuki, and I—could settle all their differences!"

"The Hebrew's words were poetry," said the delegate from Japan. "They grew, expanded, bloomed like a cherry tree. They were old wisdom."

"They were a chapter from the Christian Bible, Baron," said the American delegate. "Our Book, like the books of all the great religions, states the old truths with dignity and beauty. Those were words of our Saint Paul, who, so we think, had greater influence for the good of man than any other man, excepting Christ."

"If he who spoke to us today," said the delegate from Japan, "had been your honored saint himself, come down two thousand years to win men back to brotherhood, he scarcely could have been more eloquent. He was a fine linguist. I was fortunate to hear those great truths from your Book in my own tongue. His Japanese was absolutely flawless."

The American delegate was startled. The Russian delegate paled suddenly. "His Japanese!" The huge Slav's voice came trembling through his beard. "His Japanese! With my own ears I heard him, Baron. His speech was pure and perfect Russian."

The two turned to the delegate from America, who said nothing. "What were words? The Jew had used the Bible's beautiful and stately English. He had heard it, with his own ears!"

BIBLIOGRAPHY

WORSHIP FOR YOUNG PEOPLE

Laura Armstrong Athearn: *Christian Worship for American Youth*, The Century Co., New York.

E. L. Shaver and H. T. Stock: *Training Young People in Worship*, The Pilgrim Press, Boston.

Warren Wheeler Pickett: *Worship Services for Young People*, The Pilgrim Press, Boston.

Philip Henry Lotz: *The Quest for God Through Worship*, The Bethany Press, St. Louis, Mo.

POEMS

Henry van Dyke: *Chosen Poems*, Charles Scribner's Sons.

John Oxenham: *Gentlemen—The King*, Pilgrim Press.

John Oxenham: *The Vision Splendid.*

Clark and Gillespie: *Quotable Poems*, Vols. I and II.

T. C. Clark: *Poems of Justice.*

Angela Morgan: *Selected Poems.*

Edwin Markham: *Collected Poems.*

Boyd: *Singers of Judah's Hill.*

The Oxford Book of English Verse.

Hill: *The World's Great Religious Poetry*, Macmillan.

Mudge: *Poems with Power to Strengthen the Soul.*

SOME SOURCE BOOKS OF STORIES

Katherine Dunlap Cather: *Boyhood Stories of Famous Men*, D. Appleton-Century Co., New York.

Katherine Dunlap Cather: *Girlhood Stories of Famous Women*, D. Appleton-Century Co., New York.

Mott R. Sawyer: *Famous Friends of God*, Fleming H. Revell Co., New York.

Walter S. Erdman: *Sources of Power in Famous Lives*, Cokesbury Press, Nashville.

Walter S. Erdman: *More Sources of Power in Famous Lives*, Cokesbury Press, Nashville.

Archer Wallace: *Stories of Grit*, Doubleday, Doran Co., New York.

Fred Eastman: *Men of Power*, Cokesbury Press, Nashville.

Archer Wallace: *Overcoming Handicaps*, Doubleday, Doran Co., New York.

Margaret Eggleston: *Around the Campfire with Older Boys*, George H. Doran Co., New York.

Margaret Eggleston: *Fireside Stories for Girls in Their Teens*, Richard R. Smith, New York.

Annie Fellows Johnston: *The Jesters Sword*, L. C. Page & Co., Boston, Mass.

Jerome: *The Passing of Third Floor Back*, Dodd, Mead & Co., New York.

Basil Mathews: *Missionary Heroes*, Doubleday, Doran & Co., New York.

J. W. G. Ward: *The Glorious Galilean*, Cokesbury Press, Nashville.

Howard Pyle: *The Story of King Arthur and His Knights*, Charles Scribner's Sons, New York.

Edward Everett Hale: *The Man without a Country*, Little, Brown & Co., Boston.

Francis Jenkins Olcott: *Good Stories for Great Holidays*, Houghton Mifflin Co., Boston.

Selma Lagerlof: *Christ Legends*, Henry Holt & Co., New York.

Mabel McKee: *The Heart of the Rose*, Fleming H. Revell Co., New York.

Mary Stewart: *Tell Me a True Story*, Fleming H. Revell Co., New York.

Mary Stewart: *The Shepherd of Us All*, Fleming H. Revell Co., New York.

Henry van Dyke: *The Blue Flower*, Charles Scribner's Sons, New York.

John Ruskin: *King of the Golden River*, D. C. Heath & Co., Boston.

BIBLIOGRAPHY

Henry van Dyke: *The Toiling of Felix*, Charles Scribner's Sons, New York.

Henry van Dyke: *The Unknown Quantity*, Charles Scribner's Sons, New York.

Mary Shipman Andrews: *The Perfect Tribute*, Charles Scribner's Sons, New York.

Paul de Kruif: *Microbe Hunters*, Harcourt, Brace & Co., New York.

The Speaker, Noble and Noble, New York.

Margaret Eggleston: *Stories for Special Days in the Church School Year*, Harper & Bros., New York.

Tolstoy: *Twenty-Three Tales*, Oxford University Press, New York.

Johonnot: *Stories of the Olden Times*, American Book Co., New York.

Book of Services for Group Worship, Woman's Press, New York.

The Girl's Everyday Book, Woman's Press, New York.

Elva Smith: *Christmas in Legend and Story*, Lothrop, Lee & Shepard Co., Boston.

Costen J. Harrell: *Walking with God*, Cokesbury Press, Nashville.

A. E. Bailey: *Christ in Recent Art*, Charles Scribner's Sons, New York.

Laura I. Mattoon and Helen D. Bragdon: *Services for the Open*, D. Appleton-Century Co., New York.

Mary S. Dickie: *Singing Pathways*, Powell & White, Cincinnati.

H. Gardner: *Understanding the Arts*, Harcourt, Brace & Co., New York.

A. W. Heckman: *Paintings of Many Lands*, Art Extension Press, New York.

F. W. Ruckstuhl: *Great Works of Art and What Makes Them Great*, G. P. Putnam's Sons, New York.

Hugh Hartshorne: *Stories for Worship and How to Follow Them Up*, Charles Scribner's Sons, New York.

Basil Mathews: *Heroes in Friendship*, Oxford University Press.

Margaret Slattery: *He Took It upon Himself*, Pilgrim Press, Boston.

Henry van Dyke: *The Mansion*, Harper & Brothers, New York.

H. Augustine Smith: *Lyric Religion*, The Century Co., New York.

PRAYER

Walter Rauschenbusch: *Prayers of the Social Awakening*, Pilgrim Press, Boston.

Ralph S. Cushman: *Practicing the Presence*, Abingdon Press, New York.

Richard K. Morton: *Prayers for Young People*, Cokesbury Press, Nashville

Bertha Conde, *Spiritual Adventuring*, Cokesbury Press, Nashville.

Margaret Slattery: *A Girl's Book of Prayers*, Pilgrim Press, Boston.

Margaret Cropper: *A Prayer Book for Boys*, The Macmillan Co., New York.

John Baillie, *A Diary of Private Prayer*, Charles Scribner's Sons, New York.

Hoyland: *Prayers for Use in an Indian College*, Woman's Press, New York.

Mabel N. Thurston: *The Adventure of Prayer*, Fleming H. Revell Co., New York.

L. M. Cross: *God's Minute*, Vir Publishing Co., Philadelphia.

Harry Emerson Fosdick: *The Meaning of Prayer*, Association Press, New York.

Alfred Franklin Smith: *Talking with God*, Cokesbury Press, Nashville.

C. F. Andrews: *Christ and Prayer*.

R. W. Thomas: *We Pray Thee, Lord*, Cokesbury Press, Nashville.

STORY-TELLING

J. Berg Esenwein and Marietta Stockard: *Children's Stories and How to Tell Them*, Home Correspondence School, Springfield, Mass.

Marie L. Shedlock: *The Art of the Story-Teller*, D. Appleton & Co., New York.

Edward Porter St. John: *Stories and Story-Telling in Moral and Religious Instruction*, Pilgrim Press, Boston.

Edna Lyman: *Story-Telling—What to Tell and How to Tell It*, A. C. McClurg & Co., Chicago.

Richard T. Wyche: *Some Great Stories and How to Tell Them*, Newson & Co., New York.

Katherine Dunlap Cather: *Education by Story-Telling*, World Book Co., New York.

SOURCES OF PICTURES AND PRINTS

Artext Prints, Westport, Conn.

Art Education Press, 424 Madison Ave., New York.

F. A. Owen Publication Co., Danville, N. Y.

Perry Pictures, Malden, Mass.

Taber Prang Co., Springfield, Mass.

Rudolph Lesch Fine Arts Co., 225 Fifth Ave., New York.

W. A. Wilde Co., 131 Clarendon St., Boston.

REFERENCES AND NOTES

1 Information based upon J. Berg Esenwein and Marietta Stockard's *Children's Stories and How to Tell Them* (Manual for Story-Tellers). Used by permission.

2 Based on Psalm 43: 3; John 8: 32; 16: 13; 2 Timothy 2: 15.

3 Adapted from *Microbe Hunters*, by Paul de Kruif. Used by permission of the publishers, Harcourt, Brace and Company.

4 From *Pass On the Torch*, by Allen Eastman Cross. Used by permission of the author. (May be used as a poem if the music is not available.)

5 Based on Ecclesiasticus 44: 1-15. (A book of the Apocrypha.)

6 Adapted from "Negro Scientist Shows 'Way Out' for Southern Farmer," by Osburn Zuber, in the *Montgomery Advertiser*, December 22, 1929. Used by permission.

7 From the *International Journal of Religious Education*, April, 1936. Adapted from the prayer, "Lord, Give Me a Thirst for Truth," by Percy R. Hayward. Used by permission.

8 Based on Deuteronomy 30: 15, 16; Proverbs 3: 5, 6; 4: 23; Philippians 3: 13, 14; Hebrews 12: 1, 2.

9 From *Boyhood Stories of Famous Men*, by Katherine Dunlap Cather. Used by permission of the publishers, D. Appleton-Century Co. (Many other services may be built around the lives of other great people, such as Kagawa, Gandhi, Jacob Riis, Jane Addams, Helen Keller, Beethoven, etc.)

10 Psalm 37: 37; Matthew 5: 9; John 14: 1, 25, 27.

11 From Whittier's "The Brewing of Soma." By permission of and by arrangement with Houghton Mifflin Company.

12 From *The Children's Story Garden*, collected by a Committee of Philadelphia Yearly Meeting of Friends. Anna Pettit Broomell, Chairman. Copyright, 1920, by J. B. Lippincott Company. Used by permission.

13 From *The Vision Splendid*. Copyright, 1917, by George H. Doran Company. Used by permission of John Oxenham.

14 John 15: 12-15.

15 From *The Speaker*, published by Noble and Noble, Publishers, Inc., 100 Fifth Ave., New York City. Used by special permission.

[16] From *Quotable Poems*, Vol. 1. Used by permission of the publishers, Willett, Clark and Company.

[17] From *Stories for Special Days in the Church School Year*, by Margaret Eggleston. Used by permission of the publishers, Harper and Brothers.

[18] Psalm 8.

[19] Psalm 119: 9-11.

[20] From "The Gregorian Sacramentary," A.D. 590.

[21] From *The Blue Flower*, by Henry van Dyke; copyright, 1902, by Charles Scribner's Sons. By permission of the publishers.

[22] From "The Chambered Nautilus." Used by permission of and by arrangement with Houghton Mifflin Company.

[23] Psalm 91: 1-6; 27: 1.

[24] By Homer Greene. Used by permission of *The American Boy*.

[25] Used by permission of the author.

[26] *The New Cokesbury Hymnal*, No. 288.

[27] Psalm 15: 1, 2; Luke 13: 29; Matthew 12: 50; John 13: 35; 1 John 4: 20.

[28] Adapted from *The Secret of One Man's Power*, by L. L. Dunnington. From *Zion's Herald*, October 9, 1935. Used by permission.

[29] From *Spiritual Adventuring*, by Bertha Conde. Used by permission of the publishers, Whitmore & Smith.

[30] Ephesians 4: 6; 1 John 3: 1; Romans 12: 3-5, 10, 15, 16; Matthew 7: 2.

[31] Adapted from *The Frail Warrior*, by Jean Marie Carre. Translated from the French by Eleanor Hard. Used by permission of Coward-McCann, Inc.

[32] Used by permission of the author, Allen Eastman Cross.

[33] From *Spiritual Adventuring*, by Bertha Conde. Used by permission of the publishers, Whitmore & Smith.

[34] Luke 12: 15-21.

[35] From Tolstoy's *Twenty-Three Tales*. Used by permission of the publishers, Oxford University Press. Translation by Mr. Aylmer Maude. (An adaptation of Tolstoy's *Where Love Is, There God Is Also*, may be found in Edna Lyman's *Story-Telling*. Also in his *Twenty-Three Tales* may be found other worship material.)

[36] Matthew 5: 38-42; 7: 12.

[37] Adapted from *Les Miserables*, by Victor Hugo. Used by permission of the publishers, Ginn and Company. (Many stories may be gleaned from literature; George Eliot's *Silas Marner*; Dickens' *Tale of Two Cities*; van Dyke's *The Mansion*, or *The Story of the Other Wise Man*. In the latter story, by using the last chapter of the book, one has a shortened story for telling.)

[38] Matthew 25: 34-40.

[39] From *Ben-Hur*, by Lew Wallace. Harper and Brothers, publishers.

[40] From *Social Hymns of Brotherhood and Aspiration*, copyright, 1914, by A. S. Barnes and Company. Copyright, 1914, by Survey Associates.

[41] Psalm 1.

[42] From *Twice-Told Tales*, by Nathaniel Hawthorne. Used by permission of the publishers, Houghton Mifflin Company.

[43] By W. Angus Knight; from *Prayers for Today*, by Samuel McComb. Used by permission of the publishers, Harper and Brothers.

[44] Psalm 67.

[45] Based on Joel 2: 28; Proverbs 29: 18; Isaiah 6: 1-9.

[46] From *Quotable Poems*, Vol. II. Used by permission of the publishers, Willett, Clark and Company.

[47] Adapted from *The Passionate Pilgrim*, by Henry James. Used by permission of the publishers, Houghton Mifflin Company.

[48] Mark 10: 17-22.

[49] Reproductions of Hofmann's "Christ and the Rich Young Ruler" may be secured from Artext Prints, Westport, Conn., or from Perry Pictures Co., Malden, Mass.

[50] Used by permission of the publishers, Houghton Mifflin Company.

[51] Used by permission of the author.

[52] Based on 1 John 3: 11, 14; John 15: 12; 1 Corinthians 13; John 15: 13.

[53] May be found in *Quotable Poems*, Vol. I. Music by Effinger.

[54] From *Christian Worship for American Youth*, by Laura A. Athearn. Used by permission of the publishers, D. Appleton-Century Company. (A reproduction of "Praying Hands" large enough to use in a group may be secured from Fine Arts Co., 225 Fifth Ave., New York. Small prints may be ordered from University Prints, Boston, Mass.)

[55] By St. Ignatius Loyola.

[56] Used by permission of the author.

[57] Based on Luke 4: 18, 19; Matthew 4: 18-22; Mark 8: 34, 35.

[58] Verses which are usually omitted of the hymn, "O Jesus, I Have Promised."

[59] From *Christian Worship for American Youth*, by Laura A. Athearn. Published by the Century Company. Used by permission of the author. A reproduction of Zimmermann's "Christ and the Fishermen" may be secured from Taber Prang Company, Springfield, Mass. (A splendid packet of 16 pictures with interpretations may be ordered from Charles Scribner's Sons, 597 Fifth Avenue, New York. Bailey's *Christ in Recent Art* and Laura A. Athearn's *Christian Worship for American Youth*

contain several picture interpretations. Bailey's "Go Preach," in the Appendix, may also be used as in the above worship service.)

[60] Based on Psalms 67 and 100.

[61] Translated from the Sanskrit.

[62] Adapted from the poem "Pippa Passes," by Robert Browning.

[63] Matthew 7: 6; 6: 25, 26, 32, 33.

[64] Adapted from the poem, "The Gift of Tritemius," by Whittier. From Johonnot, *Stories of the Olden Times*. Used by permission of the publishers, The American Book Company.

[65] From *Quotable Poems,* Vol. II. Used by permission of the publishers, Willett, Clark and Company.

[66] Author unknown.

[67] Psalm 46: 1-3, 11.

[68] From Arthur C. McGiffert's *Martin Luther: The Man and His Work*. Used by permission of the publishers, D. Appleton-Century Company.

[69] Based on a story in the *Youth's Companion*. Used by permission of Franklin M. Reck, managing editor of the *American Boy*. (H. Augustine Smith's *Lyric Religion* contains material for many programs similar to the above.)

[70] *Pilgrim Hymnal* No. 118 and *Methodist Hymnal* No. 141.

[71] Psalm 93.

[72] Use the picture of "Christ at Twelve" by Hofmann, and place it so that the group will be facing it as they sing the hymn "Fairest Lord Jesus." See Bibliography for addresses of companies from whom pictures may be secured.

[73] Used by permission of the author.

[74] By St. Augustine. From the "Confessions."

[75] Matthew 9: 37, 38; John 10: 14-16; Matthew 28: 18-20.

[76] Based on the story "Oganga of the African Forest," by Hubert W. Peet, in the *World Outlook*. Used by permission.

[77] Matthew 9: 36; 10: 42; James 1: 27; Mark 12: 30, 31.

[78] Adapted from "A Modern Matriarch," by Elmer Anderson Carter, in October, 1936, *Survey Graphic*. Used by permission.

[79] From *Book of Services for Group Worship*. Used by permission of the publishers, The Woman's Press.

[80] From *Quotable Poems,* Vol. 1. Used by permission of the publishers, Willett, Clark and Company.

[81] Based upon Genesis 1: 3, 16, 6, 9, 11, 20, 26, 27.

[82] From *The Church of Lighted Lamps,* by Elizabeth Cheney. Reprinted by permission of the Methodist Book Concern.

[83] The newly elected officers should form in a semicircle, facing the leader, and stand until close of service.

[84] Candle-lighting Service should be adapted to the needs of the group.

[85] Psalm 24: 1-5.

[86] From *Tell Me a Story of Jesus,* by Mary Stewart. Used by permission of the publishers, Fleming H. Revell Co. (This book contains other splendid Bible stories. Agnes Sligh Turnbull's *Far Above Rubies* is another splendid collection of Bible stories. To give the story-teller a background for a story from the Bible read Entwistle's *The Bible Guide Book,* or E. M. Bonser's *How the Early Hebrews Lived and Learned,* or Walter Bowie's *The Story of the Bible.*)

[87] Based on Acts 17: 24-28; Psalm 104: 1, 2, 5, 6, 9, 19, 24.

[88] From *Prayers of the Social Awakening,* by Walter Rauschenbusch. Copyright by the Pilgrim Press. Used by permission.

[89] Used by permission of the author.

[90] Adapted from *The Legend of Wowassa,* by Chester L. Bower. Used by permission of the author.

[91] Based on Psalm 148: 1-3, 11-13.

[92] John 20: 1, 2, 11-18.

[93] Used by permission of the author. May be sung to the tune, "Materna."

[94] From "The Star-Promise," by Margaret Burton, taken from the *Girls' Everyday Book.* Used by permission of the publishers, the Woman's Press.

[95] By Frances Jenkins Olcott. From *The Wonder Garden.* Used by permission of the publishers, Houghton Mifflin Company.

[96] Pronounced E-van.

[97] Pronounced Va-see-ly.

[98] Acts 17: 26; Micah 4: 3; Luke 13: 29; Ephesians 2: 14.

[99] Copyright, 1935, by Whitmore and Smith, Nashville, Tenn. Used by permission of the publishers.

[100] Used by permission of Mrs. Ernest Bourner Allen.

[101] From *The Children's Story Garden,* collected by a Committee of Philadelphia Yearly Meeting of Friends. Anna Pettit Broomell, Chairman. Copyright, 1920, by J. B. Lippincott Company. Used by permission. (The story "The Tongues of Men," in the Appendix, may be substituted for this story. "Christ of the Andes" is another good peace story.)

[102] Used by permission of the author.

[103] From *Christmas in Legend and Story,* by Elva Smith. Used by permission of the publishers, Lothrop, Lee and Shepard Company. (Henry

van Dyke's *The Story of the Other Wise Man* may be substituted for the above story.)

[104] The first soloist (Traveler) should approach from the rear of the church, and the second soloist (Watchman) should stand toward the front of the church. They should be appropriately costumed and carry candled lanterns. As the Traveler sings the last stanza of the hymn he slowly approaches the front of the church so that he and the Watchman can take their places, one on each side of the tableau.

[105] For the tableau have a large picture frame (size will depend upon available space) at the front of the church, with manger, etc. At this point in the service dim the lights in the church and pull back the curtains showing Mary and Joseph looking into the manger. (From a flashlight placed in the manger have a soft light shining on Mary's face.)

[106] The Shepherds should approach from the rear of the church as they sing. They finally take their places in the tableau. The choir may join in singing as they come to the center of the church.

[107] The Wise Men approach from the rear of the church also and take their places in the tableau.

[108] If desirable, gifts may be presented at the altar at this time.

This (105-108) is an adaptation of "A Christmas Musical Service," from *Music and Worship,* by F. Fagan Thompson. Used by permission of the publishers, Whitmore and Smith.

[109] From *The Skylark's Bargain,* by G. H. Charnley. Used by permission of the publishers, Allenson & Co., London, England.

[110] Copyrighted and set to special music in *Singing Pathways,* edited by Mary S. Dickie and published by Powell and White, Cincinnati, Ohio. Used by permission of the author.

[111] Matthew 26: 41.

[112] Copyright by the Pilgrim Press. Used by permission.

[113] Based on James 1: 17; Matthew 10: 8; Luke 6: 38; Romans 12: 1, 2.

[114] Used by permission of the author, Chauncey R. Piety.

[115] Author unknown.

[116] Adapted from the hymn, "Another Year Is Dawning."

[117] Based on Matthew 6: 28, 29; Psalm 8: 3-9.

[118] Mark 7: 14, 15; Luke 6: 45; Isaiah 55: 6-9; Proverbs 16: 3.

[119] By Phebe A. Curtiss. From *What the Butterfly Learned.* Used by permission of Miss Mabel E. Curtiss.

[120] Used by permission of the author.

[121] Based on Psalm 139: 37; Matthew 5: 8.

[122] Adapted from *Walking with God,* by Costen J. Harrell. Copyright, 1930. Used by permission of the publishers, Whitmore and Smith.

[123] Used by permission of the author.

[124] Adapted from prayer, "Fourth Day (Sunday)," from *Prayers of*

the Social Awakening, by Walter Rauschenbusch. Copyright by the Pilgrim Press. Used by permission.

[125] Matthew 20: 20-28.

[126] From *The Silver Crown*, by Laura E. Richards. Used by permission of the publishers, Little, Brown and Company.

[127] Used by permission of the author.

[128] From *Spiritual Awakening*, by Bertha Conde. Used by permission of the publishers, Whitmore and Smith.

[129] Used by permission of Mrs. Robert F. Jefferys.

[130] From *The Epworth League Meeting*, by Alleen Moon. Used by permission of the publishers, Whitmore and Smith.

[131] Adapted from the poem, "The Toiling of Felix," by Henry van Dyke. Reprinted from *The Epworth League Meeting*, by Alleen Moon. Used by permission of the publishers, Whitmore and Smith.

[132] From *The Epworth League Meeting*, by Alleen Moon. Used by permission of the publishers Whitmore and Smith.

[133] Adapted from Prof. A. E. Bailey's *Christ in Recent Art*. Used by permission of the publishers, Charles Scribner's Sons.

[134] From *The Woman's Home Companion*, by R. G. Kirk. Copyright by the Crowell Publishing Co. Used by permission of the author.

INDEX OF STORIES

APPENDIX

INDEX OF HYMNS

Father in Heaven, Hear Us
A—161; T—355.

Fling Out the Banner
A—304; B—258; H—384; I—59;
M—502; P—371; T—403.

For the Beauty of the Earth
A—46; B—309; C—292; M—18;
T—16.

Go, Labor On, Spend and Be Spent
B—206; H—376; I—89; M—292;
P—330; T—285.

God of Nations Near and Far
A—296; P—380.

God of Our Youth, to Whom We
Yield
A—162.

God of Strength Enthroned Above
B—25.

God of the Earth, the Sky, the Sea
A—49.

God of the Strong, God of the
Weak
A—212; M—457.

God Send Us Men Whose Aim
'Twill Be
A—255 I—224; P—323.

God the Omnipotent
A—284; H—420; I—194; M—505.

God's Trumpet Wakes the Slumbering World
A—203; M—262; P—260.

Gracious Spirit, Dwell with Me
I—159; H—214; P—186.

Great Master, Touch Us
A—222; I—295; P—162.

Heaven Is Here, Where Hymns of
Gladness
A—240; M—461.

Heralds of Christ
A—258 H—379; I—383; M—482;
P—375; T—407.

Holy, Holy, Holy
A—4; B—1; C—158; H—57; I—3;
M—1; P—1 T—1.

Holy Spirit, Truth Divine
A—60; H—208; I—319; M—173;
P—496.

Honor and Glory, Power and
Salvation
M—16; P—17.

I Thank Thee, Lord, for Life
A—166.

I Would Be True
A—177; I—158; P—469.

If I Can Stop One Heart from
Breaking
A—242.

In Life's Earnest Morning
A—213.

Jesus Calls Us, O'er the Tumult
A—144; B—188; H—223; I—28;
M—233; P—152; T—284.

Jesus, Saviour, Pilot Me
A—160; B—238; C—270; H—286;
I—53; M—269; P—284; T—235.

Jesus Shall Reign
A—305; B—260; C—219; H—377;
I—21; M—479; P—373; T—392.

Jesus, the Very Thought of Thee
A—158; B—139; C—353; H—309;
I—112; M—348; P—150; T—76.

O Thou Whose Feet Have Climbed
C—214; M—559; T—329

O Worship the King
A—36; B—34; C—294; H—2; I—15; M—4; P—5; T—7.

O Young and Fearless Prophet
M—266.

O Zion, Haste
A—306; B—264; C—224; M—475; T—395.

Open My Eyes
I—324.

Pass on the Torch
A—229.

Praise the Lord
A—30; B—38; C—300; H—10; I—254; M—11; P—7; T—10.

Purer Yet and Purer
B—192; I—129; T—260.

Rejoice, Ye Pure in Heart
A—27; B—47; H—297; I—99; M—358; P—476.

Saviour, Again to Thy Dear Name
A—24; B—22; C—437; M—29; T—451.

Silent Night, Holy Night
A—81; C—530; H—132; I—72; M—100; P—98; T—60.

Spirit of God, Descend upon My Heart
A—62; B—150; H—204; I—110; M—179; P—233; T—125.

Stand Up, Stand Up for Jesus
A—201; B—205, 365; H—265; I—14; M—283; P—507; T—288.

Take Thou Our Minds
H—245.

Teach Me, My God and King
C—262; M—320; P—193.

The Body, Lord, Is Ours to Keep
A—164.

The King of Love My Shepherd Is
A—50; B—224; C—345; H—99; I—96; M—353; P—287; T—80.

The Light of God Is Falling
H—400; M—468; P—309; T—376.

The Spacious Firmament
A—47; B—53; H—69; I—144; M—66; P—160; T—8.

The Voice of God Is Calling
M—454; P—337.

There's a Wideness in God's Mercy
A—55; B—64; C—256; H—93; I—192; M—76; P—180; T—18.

This Is My Father's World
A—39; B—406; H—70; I—226; M—72; P—464; T—332.

Thou Who Taught the Thronging People
A—113; P—116.

To the Knights in the Days of Old
A—230; I—379.

Watchman, Tell Us of the Night
A—298; B—263; H—109; I—126; M—485; P—70; T—393.

We Thank Thee, Lord, Thy Paths
A—249; H—367; M—458; P—340.

We Three Kings of Orient Are
A—96; I—241; M—102; P—101.

Where Cross the Crowded Ways of Life
A—265 B—276; C—235; H—410; I—61; M—465; P—140; T—330.